THE CONCISE
LEADERSHIP
TEXTBOOK

"Professor Pittino has produced a strong and much-needed guide to leadership that provides clear, concise and key information in a highly accessible way for the busy person. This is a very timely book and will assist a wide range of audiences including executives, students, policy-makers, and consultants. A text to have by your side."

Professor Peter Strokes, Professor of Leadership and Professional Development,
De Montfort University (UK)

"This is a book I wish I had written. In a clear and lucid manner, Daniel Pittino has done a masterful job of presenting the theory and practice of leadership. If you're a rookie leader, or an experienced one looking to stay on course, this is the book for you. Its brevity promotes clarity, insight, and ultimately right action."

Louise Kelly, PhD, Professor of Management, University of La Verne (California),
author of the *Dictionary of Strategy* and the *Psychologist Manager*

"Daniel Pittino skillfully intertwines leadership research, case studies, and self-reflection while delivering an engaging and unpretentious read. Few leadership books can claim comprehensive coverage of the field and practice of leadership, so it is unexpected that such a brief textbook has achieved this. Anyone interested in honing, growing or coaching leadership skills will appreciate the concise and effective personal development activities peppered seamlessly throughout. I encourage everyone to read this book."

Charmine E. J. Härtel, Ph.D., Associate Dean Research Impact,
Professor and Director, The Opportunity Tech Lab, Inclusive Leadership & Entrepreneurship,
Monash Business School, Monash University (Australia)

"Daniel Pittino presents a punchy yet detailed examination of leadership. He brilliantly weaves together research, examples, thoughtful figures, and short exercises to create a succinct book that is well-suited to students, professionals, and executives desiring to know more about leadership. The Concise Leadership Textbook is a masterclass in making progress together with other people—the measure of a good leader."

Mathew (Mat) Hughes, Ph.D., Schulze Distinguished Professor,
Professor of Entrepreneurship and Innovation, Loughborough University (UK)

THE CONCISE
LEADERSHIP
TEXTBOOK

ESSENTIAL KNOWLEDGE AND SKILLS FOR
DEVELOPING YOURSELF AS A LEADER

DANIEL PITTINO

econcise
Concise books for smart learners

Our mission at econcise publishing
is to create concise, approachable and affordable
textbooks for a new generation of smart learners.

Paperback ISBN: 978-3-903386-09-9
ePub ISBN: 978-3-903386-10-5
Kindle ISBN: 978-3-903386-11-2

Copy editor: Harriet Power
Cover design: Farrukh_bala
Cover/back cover image, paper plane illustration on pp. 5, 25, 55, 83, 109: iStock.com/Dmitry Volkov
People icons on pp. 8, 46, 49, 62, 66, 68, 90, 110: iStock.com/Ville Heikkinnen
Illustration elements:
 • p. 49 and p. 90: iStock.com/da-vooda
 • p. 66: iStock.com/Nikolamirejovska
 • p. 90: iStock.com/artvea, iStock.com/in8finity, iStock.com/Shendart
 • p. 101: iStock.com/Peacefully7, iStock.com/fonikum, iStock.com/in8finity, pixabay.com

First published 2022 by **econcise publishing**
© 2022 econcise GmbH
Am Sonnengrund 14
A-9062 Moosburg (Austria)

www.econcise.com

Contents

Chapter 4: Contemporary leadership challenges

Chapter 5: Leadership tools and techniques

Introduction

Are you looking for a short, clear and actionable, yet research-based, approach to the topic of leadership as a student? Are you interested in **developing leadership competences and skills** in your professional role or for your future career? Are you willing to learn about the implications of leadership in your everyday life and in the face of an increasingly complex world?

Then *The Concise Leadership Textbook* is the right book for you!

Leadership is a vast and multifaceted topic, supported by an enormous amount of scientific studies and theories, with equally huge practical implications. So it is easy to feel overwhelmed as you try to learn more about it. You may also be confused about which paths to follow to grow as a leader. You may even think that "leadership is for someone else, but not for me."

This book will help you overcome these concerns.

The Concise Leadership Textbook offers **a compact yet comprehensive overview of the foundational knowledge about leadership**. It also provides you with guidelines for applying that knowledge in the development of leadership competences including the most important aspects of leadership in relation to contemporary challenges.

This is supported by an approach that combines **solid research-based knowledge, practical applications** and **tested methods** to transform that knowledge into effective leadership action, and **best-practice insights** from successful leadership cases.

Throughout the book, you will also find **exercises** and '**Build your leadership skills' boxes** that you can use to develop and strengthen your own leadership skillset.

Here is a short overview of what you will learn in the five chapters of this book:

- In **Chapter 1** *(What is leadership?)*, you will explore what leadership is all about; compare different perspectives on the study of leadership; understand the connection between leadership and the ability to solve 'wicked' problems; and distinguish between management and leadership.
- In **Chapter 2** *(Know yourself: Leadership traits, skills, and behaviors)*, you will learn about the importance of self-awareness as a basic leadership skill; explore the link between different personality traits and effective leadership; reflect on which problem-solving, human, and technical skills you need to develop to perform well in a leadership role; and assess the impact of different leadership styles and behaviors on your effectiveness as a leader.
- In **Chapter 3** *(How to lead (with) others)*, you will learn about leadership as problem solving with other people (your followers); recognize the link between your followers' characteristics and different types of leadership behavior and leadership results; explore how you can help your team members develop, learn, and grow with a transformational leadership approach; identify the key aspects that determine your team performance; and assess the benefits and risks of a shared leadership approach.
- In **Chapter 4** *(Contemporary leadership challenges)*, you will learn about leadership in a global context and reflect on the specific requirements of leading virtual teams; recognize the importance of ethics in your leadership attitude and actions; identify the main leadership competences for more sustainable and inclusive organizations and society; and learn how to lead change processes in both relatively stable and highly dynamic environments.
- In **Chapter 5** *(Leadership tools and techniques)*, you will familiarize yourself with some useful techniques that support your development as a leader. Specifically, you will learn about effective leadership communication; get insights on how to prepare and deliver an engaging leadership speech; discover which decision-making style is the best fit in specific situations; analyze and choose differ-

ent approaches to managing and resolving conflicts; learn coaching techniques to help followers develop themselves; and create your own leadership development plan.

You can see the chapters of this book as a map for your personal journey into leadership development. Let this map guide you to find your own path to becoming an effective leader.

Always keep in mind, however, that leadership is about **making progress together with other people**. The ultimate measure of a good leader is not only achieving set goals, but also gaining recognition and appreciation from your followers.

> *"As a team, we would like to thank you for being so supportive and engaging during this project. Thank you for being the best team leader!"*

> *"It's great to be recognized for my hard work and dedication. Your thoughtfulness and generosity empower me and encourage me to do my best!"*

> *"Thank you for your vision and your leadership guiding us at all times. We really appreciate your efforts!"*

With the help of this textbook, I truly hope that you will go on to receive rewarding feedback like that reflected in the quotes above.

Welcome to the exciting journey of growing as a leader, and welcome to *The Concise Leadership Textbook*!

ACCESS FREE BONUS LEARNING MATERIALS

Learn smarter with our free additional learning resources that accompany *The Concise Leadership Textbook*!

Both learners and lecturers can access the following additional learning materials in the 'Smart Learning' section on the book's companion website at *www.econcise.com/ConciseLeadershipTextbook*:

- **Mind maps** that provide a succinct, visual 'big picture' overview of the key concepts in each chapter.
- **Links to videos and additional resources** related to selected topics in the book.
- **Interactive flashcards** for a quick revision of the key concepts in each chapter.

If you are a lecturer, send us an email to *lecturerservice@econcise.com*. We can then provide you with editable **PowerPoint slides** for each chapter of this book and a set of **multiple-choice questions** for your exams.

If you want to stay informed about current developments in the field and get more information about new books for smart learners, you are also welcome to visit *www.econcise.com/newsletter* and subscribe to our newsletter!

What is leadership?

This chapter will enable you to:

» Describe what leadership is all about.
» Compare different perspectives on the study of leadership.
» Recognize the link between leadership and the ability to solve 'wicked' problems.
» Distinguish between management and leadership.

The topic of leadership has fascinated humanity across the centuries. Great leaders have been admired and celebrated for making the fortunes of nations, as well as for promoting the progress of social, religious, and economic organizations. Throughout history, however, some leaders have also been responsible for dramatic failures and disastrous consequences.

Given its great potential, both as a positive and negative force, leadership is of utmost importance at every level of society. Good, positive leadership is needed to solve the increasingly complex problems that emerge at the global scale, as well as in everyday life and work, within companies, communities, teams, associations, or in any other form of human collaboration.

But what do we mean when we talk about leadership?

Defining leadership

Over the last hundred years, during which leadership has become a consolidated subject of study by scientists in various fields, many definitions have been proposed for the concept of 'leadership'.[1] These definitions are often very different, reflecting diverse analytical but also cultural and ethical viewpoints. It is therefore difficult to develop a conclusive description of the concept of leadership.

For the purposes of this book, we will adopt a definition that relies on common aspects shared by most of the previous characterizations of leadership. We'll **define leadership** as:

> *A process of social influence aimed at reaching a common goal within a group or an organization.*

This definition highlights some key aspects:[2]

- Leadership is a **process**, meaning that it is not simply a 'static' and formal attribute of a person, but a series of actions and interactions that are oriented toward achieving certain results.
- Leadership occurs through **social influence**, meaning that it involves a relationship between leaders and followers. Followers are influenced by the leader, but they can also influence the leader. The ability to influence others is usually associated with having some form of power.
- Leadership is a deliberate, voluntary process which **aims to reach a goal** based on a shared purpose among the members of a group or an organization.
- The presence of a common goal stresses the fact that **leadership needs followership**; leaders need followers and work with them to achieve the common purpose.

Based on the points above, we can identify the **leader** as the person guiding the process of social influence toward the common goal.

It is important to note that the leader can be a single individual in charge of every stage of the process, but there could also be multiple leaders for different phases of the process or for different problems that need to be solved together. Shared (or joint) leadership within the group is therefore possible too (we will further explain this aspect later in this book).

Having a formal position of power in a business or an organization (e.g. in the role of a CEO, president, director, or manager) is only one—and not necessarily the most important—aspect of leadership. This is because the social influence that occurs in the leadership process can come from various sources. These '**sources of power**' can be classified into:[3]

- **Referent power**: based on viewing the leader as a reference point and as a person with whom followers can identify.
- **Expert power**: based on the leader's competence and/or expertise in specific fields.
- **Legitimate power**: associated with holding a position that entails formal job authority.
- **Reward power**: comes from the capacity to provide rewards to followers.
- **Coercive power**: derives from the capacity to penalize or punish followers.
- **Information power**: derives from having exclusive access to information or knowledge that is important for others.

The **influence** exerted by a leader on others—the effect that a leader has on their opinions, beliefs, and/or behaviors—is usually a combination of several of these sources of power.

EXERCISE

EXPLORING THE BEHAVIOR OF EFFECTIVE AND INEFFECTIVE LEADERS

Think about a situation where you have been a follower of an effective leader (e.g. at work, during your studies, in a sports team, or in any other situation in which you were part of a group that wanted to achieve something together). List three features that you appreciated in this leader or leadership situation.

Now think about a situation where you have been a follower of an ineffective leader. List three features that you did not appreciate in this leader or leadership situation.

Differing perspectives on leadership

The key features of leadership summarized in our definition above have been studied through various lenses or perspectives (see Figure 1.1 for an overview).

Let us take a closer look at each of these perspectives, since each of them has important implications for leadership education, practice, and development.

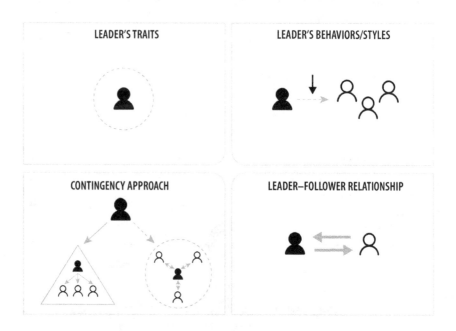

Figure 1.1 Different perspectives on studying leadership

The leader's traits

The study of leadership based on individual traits focuses on the **attributes of leaders such as personality, skills and abilities, motivation, or values.**

Historically, this approach has its origins in the 1930s and assumes that leaders possess distinctive characteristics which are not present in 'ordinary' people. These characteristics have been identified, for example, in above-average intelligence, extraordinary energy, intuition, self-confidence, physical appearance, or specific values and beliefs.[4]

The assumption underlying this view of leadership is that some people are born with certain attributes that make them **'natural leaders'**— great and charismatic individuals who are capable of achieving successful outcomes—and that these attributes are absent or less pronounced in 'non-leaders.'

The 'trait' approach has progressively been abandoned, mainly because:

- it has failed to identify a 'one best way,' a conclusive list of traits that are consistently associated with effective leadership,
- it ignores the role of other social factors, including the organizational context, the experiences of the leader, and the characteristics of the followers,
- it seems to neglect the possibility of 'becoming' a leader through learning and practice, and
- it tends to overlook the actual behaviors of the leader.[5]

Some of these criticisms have been addressed in more recent rediscoveries of the trait approach, in particular by research focusing more on skills and competences related to work performance and problem solving.[6]

Leadership behavior and styles

The **leadership behavior** perspective addresses one of the main limitations of the trait approach, namely its narrow focus on 'who leaders are' and scarce attention on 'what leaders actually do.'

This approach is concerned with understanding, through empirical observation, which recurrent types of leadership behavior (often labelled as **'leadership styles'**) can be linked to certain performance outcomes.

One of the pioneers in defining leadership behavioral styles was the social psychologist Kurt Lewin.[7] In 1939, he defined three **behavioral styles of a leader:**

- **Autocratic,** where the leader defines and supervises work goals, methods, and plans, and makes decisions with little or no involvement from others.

- **Participative**, where the leader defines priorities and goals, but is open to group discussion and suggestions when it comes to implementing and adjusting the goals.
- **Delegative** (sometimes also called 'laissez-faire' in its extreme form), where the leader hands over to the group the responsibility for organizing the work and attaining results.

A decade after this early definition of leadership styles, which is still widely used and referred to in practice, a more systematic series of studies was conducted, first by a group of researchers based at Ohio State University,[8] followed by researchers at Michigan State University.[9] These studies suggest that leadership is characterized by two general types of behaviors, namely:

- **task-oriented behaviors** that facilitate goal accomplishment by the group, and
- **relationship-oriented behaviors** that promote the individual and social well-being of group members.

Other studies, as well as applications of leadership behavioral styles, basically elaborate on these two behavioral types with more or less sophisticated classifications. Arguably the most famous of these classifications of leadership styles is the one proposed by **Blake and Mouton** in the 1960s.[10]

Their classification is based on two dimensions: **concern for people** and **concern for production**. These dimensions jointly define five basic leadership styles:

1. **Country club style** (high concern for people, low concern for production)
2. **Produce or perish style** (low concern for people, high concern for production)
3. **Impoverished style** (low concern for both people and production)
4. **Middle-of-the-road style** (medium concern for both people and production)
5. **Team leadership style** (high concern for both people and production)

You will learn more about these styles in Chapter 2, along with other aspects of leaders' behavior and their practical implications.

The behavioral approach also has its **shortcomings**: first, the categories of leader behavior are generally too broadly defined, which leads to a lack of consistent research results on the link between leadership styles and performance outcomes. Second, similar to the trait approach, the behavioral approach aims to identify behavioral patterns that represent a 'one best way' for leadership—a goal that both approaches fail to achieve.

The contingency approach

The 'one best way' view of leadership is abandoned with the **contingency approach**, which focuses on contextual factors that influence the relationship between leadership behaviors and outcomes (for example, in terms of the satisfaction of group members and group performance).

Various **contextual factors** have been considered within the contingency approach, the most relevant being:

- the nature of work tasks performed by the group or unit under the responsibility of the leader,
- the type of organization where the leader operates,
- the characteristics of the external environment, and
- the characteristics of the followers.

The contingency approach has been used to discover which aspects of the surrounding situation influence a leader's behavior. It has also been used to find out more about which leadership attributes and behaviors are more effective in different situations.

The assumption underlying this approach is that **leadership styles and behaviors should be adapted to match the situation**, which is defined by various aspects that may change over time and across different settings (for example, different types of companies, different characteristics of the followers, or different conditions in terms of uncertainty).

The contingency approach is used extensively in leadership development, mainly through the **Situational Leadership Model**, developed in the 1960s by behavioral scientists and consultants Paul Hersey and Ken

Blanchard,[11] and through the **path–goal theory**, proposed by the psychologist Fred E. Fiedler in the same period.[12]

A contingency approach has also been adopted in more recent contextual classifications of leadership styles, for example the **six emotional leadership styles** proposed by Daniel Goleman, Richard Boyatzis, and Annie McKee.[13] The six styles are:

1. **Commanding**: telling people what they have to do
2. **Visionary**: inspiring people with a compelling idea of a better future for the organization
3. **Affiliative**: leading through creating strong personal relationships and a team spirit
4. **Democratic**: fostering dialogue and joint decision making
5. **Pacesetting**: with a strong focus on performance, setting challenging goals, and achieving short-term results
6. **Coaching**: developing people and their strengths with a long-term perspective

Each of these styles is particularly appropriate in certain situations and not in others. You will find an application of the six styles proposed by Goleman and colleagues in Chapter 4.

The contingency approach, despite being widely used, may sometimes suffer from excessive complexity (due to the many variables involved), which limits its practical application. At the same time, there are always some potential contingent factors that may be overlooked, thus making the models potentially less effective.

The approaches focusing on the leader–followers relationship

The prominent management theorist Peter Drucker provided a famous definition of leadership as simply "having followers."[14] More recent perspectives on leadership have placed increasing attention on the **role of followers** and on the relationship between leaders and followers.

Within this approach we could further differentiate between:

1. views that are more centered around **leaders' values that appeal to followers**, and
2. views that are more focused on the **interaction between leader and followers**.

The first group of views belongs to the so-called 'value-based approach.'[15] In this approach, followers are drawn to identify with the leader's values and emulate the leader's behavior, because they feel inspired and motivated by the idealized vision proposed by the leader.

There are many examples of concepts and theories falling into this view, for example:

- **Transformational leadership**: emphasizes the followers being inspired by and identifying with a higher purpose envisioned by the leader.
- **Neo-charismatic leadership**: similar to transformational leadership, as it stresses the role of the leader in inspiring followers to embrace change.
- **Ethical leadership**: helps individuals behave according to values that promote a common good for the organization and/or for society.
- **Authentic leadership**: emphasizes honest, transparent, and open behavior, especially in accepting followers' inputs in decision making.
- **Spiritual leadership**: vision, hope and altruism are driving factors.
- **Servant leadership**: the primary responsibility and motivation of a leader is serving others, by focusing on the needs of others and on the collective purpose as a greater good.

The second group of views is more **'follower-centered'** in the sense that they are interested in how the relationship between leaders and followers is built (particularly seen from the followers' point of view).

One example comes from the **leader–member exchange theory** (also known as the **LMX theory**), which identifies two types of social exchange that may occur between leaders and followers.[16] The first type is defined as 'in-group exchange' and identifies a high-quality relationship, characterized by mutual trust, loyalty, and shared purpose. The second type, 'out-group exchange,' is characterized by a lower quality relationship, which relies on control and formal expectations. The followers may belong to either the 'in-group' or the 'out-group,' and which group they belong to has a direct influence on their performance.

Another example of this perspective is the view of **leadership as social construction**.[17] According to this view, leadership is not something that is given 'once and for all,' for instance to someone holding a formal position, but instead has to be built and continuously maintained through a process of exchange between followers and leader, whereby leaders 'claim' their position through ongoing actions and messages, and followers 'grant' or 'withdraw' support to the leader with their own actions and messages.

You will learn more about the application of the concepts developed within the leader–follower approach in Chapter 3.

EXERCISE

APPLYING THE FOUR PERSPECTIVES ON LEADERSHIP

Referring to the features of effective and ineffective leaders that you listed in the previous exercise, try to classify them using the four perspectives (traits, behaviors and styles, contextual factors, and relationships with the followers).

For example, if you appreciated the extroverted character of an effective leader, this is mainly an aspect related to the traits perspective.

Leadership and effectiveness: solving wicked problems

The perspectives on leadership that we summarized in the previous section have one thing in common: the focus on what determines leadership effectiveness. This is connected to a key question: when and to what extent does leadership really affect organizational behaviors and performance?

There is a stream of research suggesting that organizations, both in business and society, are influenced by powerful **forces that limit the actual impact of leaders.**[18] These factors are both internal (for example, organizational structure) and external (for example, characteristics of the industry and market forces), and act as constraints on the decision making and actions of the organizational leaders.

This resonates with the so-called 'deterministic views' in literature and philosophy. Writer Leo Tolstoy, for example, contended that leaders are only by chance associated with great events in history, and in fact it is history that determines the course of events, with individuals having little true impact, despite being regarded as 'great' men or women.

On the other hand, research in business and management has also shown that **leadership matters for the effectiveness of organizations** by having a significant impact on their economic performance. In particular, recent studies show that the impact of CEOs on financial performance has increased substantially in the past few decades. For example, a study based on US data spanning 60 years and more than 18,000 observations across 30 industries shows that the effect of business leaders on firm performance has doubled in the last 30 years to around 20 percent, which makes a substantial impact.[19]

Other evidence shows that leadership has the highest impact on effectiveness when organizations operate in **complex situations**, characterized by competition, turbulence and hard-to-spot opportunities.[20] Complex situations involve a number of 'wicked problems' that can be solved only through proper leadership.

Leadership expert Keith Grint proposed the idea that there are different types of problems that require different responses.[21] He makes a distinction between tame, critical, and wicked problems (see Figure 1.2).

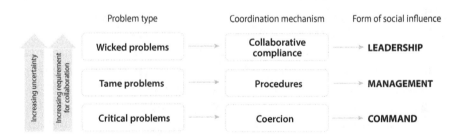

Figure 1.2 Types of problems and approaches to solving them[22]

Tame problems are those that have known causes and can be solved by applying known processes and predefined procedures or rules. An example of a tame problem is a production process that needs to be scaled up to meet increased demand. The required approach for addressing tame problems is a typical 'management' one, in the sense that problems are solved through the optimization of already established structures and processes. Basically, this means 'doing the same things in a better way.'

Solving tame problems can be very complicated, as it may involve very sophisticated skills and require the application of advanced knowledge—think about heart surgery, for example. But ultimately it remains a technical problem that is tackled through the perfect execution of predefined rules and procedures.

Critical problems emerge when there is a crisis that may threaten the continuity and survival of an organization. Critical problems call for short-term action and present little ambiguity or uncertainty over what needs to be done. Since action is expected in a short timeframe, it is not possible to apply known procedures, for example to perform an objective analysis and identify optimal solutions, as in the case of tame problems. Instead, solutions may follow statements of fact that are assumed to be valid, or pressing requests from the external environment.

Examples of critical problems are corporate scandals that involve unethical and/or illegal company behavior, emergencies that disrupt business operations, and responses to accidents, natural disasters, or terrorist attacks. Critical problems typically require a 'command' approach that involves rapid and unquestioned execution of orders, coercion, and tight control of people.

Wicked problems are different from the previous two since they do not have known causes and predefined solutions (as in the case of tame problems), and it is also not possible to make assumptions about actions that are unquestionably needed to solve the problem (as in the case of critical problems).

Examples of wicked problems are finding appropriate responses to the public health emergency caused by the COVID-19 pandemic, addressing climate change, or, at the company level, pursuing environmentally sustainable strategies with limited resources and multiple economic and social constraints (e.g. staying cost-competitive and preserving occupational levels at the same time).

The concept of wicked problems first appeared in the work of two professors of design and urban planning at the University of California at Berkeley, Horst W. J. Rittel and Melvin M. Webber.[23] They gave the following **defining characteristics of a wicked problem:**

- **Wicked problems cannot be described or 'formulated' in a definitive way.** The explanations of a wicked problem vary greatly depending on the individual's perspective. As a consequence, wicked problems do not have a predetermined number of potential solutions, and you cannot have a final test for a solution to a wicked problem.
- **There is no 'stopping rule' for a wicked problem:** no way to know whether your solution is final. The decision maker may instead stop when they feel that a solution is 'good enough,' one they 'like,' or 'the best that can be done given the constraints of the situation.' It is impossible to classify solutions to wicked problems as true or false. We can only evaluate whether they are good or bad, better or worse, satisfying, or 'good enough.'
- Due to a lack of opportunity to learn through experimenting (a trial-and-error approach does not work for wicked problems), **solutions to wicked problems are 'one-shot operations.'** This is also because every wicked problem is new and, as Rittel and Weber say, "essentially unique." You can learn only partially from apparently similar problems.

These characteristics are common to many problems in organizations and society. In fact we could argue that the number and variety of wicked problems is rapidly increasing at all levels, due to economic, social, and technological transformations occurring at a growing pace.

Wicked problems can only be addressed through leadership, by **guiding a process of social influence involving collaboration, shared goals, and joint problem solving.** We can say that leadership effectiveness can be ultimately assessed by the ability to work with wicked problems.

LEADERS WHO ARE EFFECTIVE IN ADDRESSING WICKED PROBLEMS[24]

Professors Natalia Karelaia and Ludo Van der Heyden from INSEAD analyzed remarkable examples of leaders dealing effectively with wicked problems. New Zealand's prime minister Jacinda Ardern, Germany's chancellor Angela Merkel, and Michigan's governor Gretchen Whitmer all understood the crucial role of collective commitment in the challenging situation of the COVID-19 outbreak. Karelaia and Van der Heyden highlighted what those leaders had in common in their actions and identified five phases for dealing with wicked problems.

- **Phase 1: Framing the problem.** The first step consists of clearly identifying the problem that has to be solved. This orients efforts toward the right goal, without creating 'fake enemies' or wasting time and energy in short-term responses. In this phase, the leader should not be afraid to ask a lot of questions, on a very broad scope. Asking questions allows the leader to involve others in the leadership process. By doing this the leader builds an accurate understanding of the problem and at the same time creates collective commitment. Examples of questions to be asked at this stage are: What kind of problem are we facing? What will happen if we do not act now? Has someone encountered this kind of problem and developed solutions before? What are the requirements and implications of possible solutions?
- **Phase 2: Patiently exploring the options.** In the case of wicked problems, due to the uncertainty that characterizes them, embracing the first solution is usually not the best idea. Instead, many possible options should be generated and explored, because in this way the leader will get a thorough understanding of the problem and improve the credibility and effectiveness of the solution. The exploration of potential options will benefit greatly from the involvement of others, in a group effort.

- **Phase 3: Taking a firm decision and clearly explaining the motivation behind it.** The leader needs to be decisive in choosing a course of action from the possible solutions that have been explored. At the same time, the leader has to be prepared to explain the decision in depth, and communicate with honesty their expectations for the solution. This process is strengthened if the leader engages in debates with multiple opinions, where helpful suggestions and challenging critiques emerge. If the two previous phases have been completed successfully, the leader is more likely to have the confidence that is required in this phase. When making a decision, the leader should balance and combine empathy and understanding with facts and rational analysis.
- **Phase 4: Executing with commitment.** In situations that involve great uncertainty, the selected decision has to be pursued with determination to have the best chance of success. The leader should continue to explain their reasoning and the expectations, but not engage any longer in debates that question the value of the solution implemented. The time for debates can be extensive, but they have a place in phases 1 and 2 only. Maximum commitment has to be given to the chosen solution, as long as that solution is considered to be the right one. If the solution does not prove to be effective, the leader must be ready to admit that it doesn't work and move on. They should not fall into the trap of persevering in a course of action that is clearly deemed to fail.
- **Phase 5: Assessing the outcomes, learning to adapt, and starting again.** The leader should engage in progress reviews that compare actual results with expectations. The leader needs to explain honestly and transparently what was successful and what was not, and what has been learned.

A LEADER WITH A WICKED PROBLEM

Reflect on a situation that you have experienced where a leader (this could be you or someone else) has faced a wicked problem.

Identify the characteristics of the problem that made it a wicked one and answer the following questions:

- How did the leader act in tackling the wicked problem?
- What worked well?
- What could have been done better?

Leadership and management

Leadership and management are often used as interchangeable terms. This is due to the fact that they share a lot of common aspects. For example, both involve influencing other people, both are concerned with accomplishing goals, and both happen mostly in organized social contexts. Furthermore, individuals who occupy management positions are often required to assume leadership responsibility.

Beyond the similarities and overlaps, however, there are also some important differences between the two. As pointed out by the prominent leadership scholar Peter G. Northouse, the interest in studying leadership dates back to ancient Greece, with Plato and Aristotle, whereas management as a discipline only emerged during the 19th and 20th centuries, in parallel with the advent of industrialization.[25]

Management was created as a tool to make organizations run more effectively and efficiently. The **core functions of management** were identified by the French engineer and business theorist Henri Fayol in 1916 as **planning, organizing, staffing, and controlling.**[26] These functions are ultimately related to the 'technical' aspects of problem solving, which are best applied to tame problems.

If the overall aim of management is to ensure order and consistency in existing activities, **leadership is primarily concerned with future goals and change**. In other words, management is usually more focused on efficiency (or, in Peter Drucker's words, "doing the things right"), whereas leadership is more about what Drucker called "doing the right things," and effectively contributing to fulfilling an important purpose.[27]

A study involving experts in management and organizational psychology on the competences associated with leadership and management reveals that the competences that are distinctive for leadership include motivating intrinsically, creative thinking, strategic planning, tolerance of ambiguity, and people reading. Conversely, management is best described by competences such as short-term planning, motivating extrinsically, orderliness, timeliness, and rule orientation.[28]

Unlike management, leadership has an impact on organizational performance that is not necessarily direct, but instead occurs by **influencing the context in which people work**. This means that effective leadership acts on dimensions such as organizational culture, organizational climate, and employee engagement.[29]

Organizational culture can be understood as 'the way things are done' in an organization and represents the assumptions, values and beliefs that are shared among people working in that organization.[30] **Organizational climate** refers to 'how it feels,' namely how employees perceive the work environment. Research has shown that effective leadership influences the quality of an organization by having a direct effect on both culture and climate.[31] Both culture and climate also appear to be closely associated with the loyalty and satisfaction of employees, which, in turn, translate into positive performance outcomes.[32]

In light of this it becomes clear that **organizations need both leadership and management**. An organization that has strong leadership but poor management becomes incapable of translating visions and ideas into consistent outcomes. An organization which has strong management but poor leadership becomes rigid and excessively bureaucratic, and is unable to cope with change and transformation.

ARE YOU A MANAGER OR LEADER?

Go through the questions below and choose answers 'A' or 'B' to find out whether you are more oriented toward managing or leading.

	Question	A	B
1	Which task is generally easier for you?	*Setting clear, measurable goals*	*Creating a vision of what the future will look like*
2	Which kind of situation do you feel more comfortable in?	*When the situation remains stable*	*When the situation is constantly changing*
3	What are you better at?	*Understanding structured reports*	*Understanding other people's emotions*
4	What is your attitude toward conflict?	*Conflict should best be avoided*	*Conflict is important for making progress*
5	How do you feel about uncertainty and ambiguity?	*I prefer things to be clear, unambiguous and certain*	*I have a high tolerance for ambiguity and uncertainty*
6	In your opinion, which is the better way to make sure that people in your team are performing well in their tasks?	*Control them*	*Trust them*
7	What is your attitude toward risk-taking?	*I try to control and minimize risks wherever possible*	*I am happy to take risks*
8	What are you better at?	*Developing structures and processes*	*Shaping the culture of the team*
9	In your opinion, which of the two statements is a better description of how to ensure that people perform well in their work?	*People are more likely to perform well when they have clear rules to follow*	*People are more likely to perform well when they know the purpose of their work*

After answering the questions, count how many 'A' and 'B' answers you have selected. If you have chosen more 'A' answers, you hold more of a management attitude. More 'B' answers indicate that you have already adopted a leadership attitude.

WHAT IS LEADERSHIP?
A BRIEF SUMMARY IN 10 POINTS

1. Leadership is a **process of social influence aimed at reaching a common goal within a group or an organization**.

2. **Power is a crucial part of the influence process** and can be classified into referent power, expert power, legitimate power, reward power, coercive power, and information power.

3. The **key features of leadership** have been studied adopting **various perspectives**: the leaders' traits approach, the leaders' behaviors and styles approach, the contingency view of leadership, and the approach focusing on the leaders–followers relationship.

4. The study of leadership based on individuals' traits focuses on the **attributes of leaders** such as personality, skills and abilities, motivation, and values.

5. The study of **leadership behavior** focuses on '**what leaders actually do**' and is concerned with identifying, through empirical observation, recurrent behaviors that can be grouped into leadership styles.

6. The **contingency view** focuses on the **contextual factors** that influence the relationship between the leader's behaviors and outcomes.

7. The focus on the **leader–followers relationship** has two facets: views that are more centered around leaders' values that appeal to followers, and views that are more focused on the interaction between leader and followers.

8. All the perspectives on leadership have one thing in common: the focus on **what determines leadership effectiveness**. Leadership effectiveness is mainly related to the ability to solve wicked problems.

9. **Wicked problems**, which are very frequent in contemporary organizations and society, are problems that have numerous interconnected causes and no predefined solutions. Wicked problems are different from critical problems that can be solved through a 'coercive approach' and tame problems that can be solved through a 'management approach.'

10. The ability to deal with wicked problems **differentiates leadership from management**. The aim of management is to ensure order and consistency in existing activities, while leadership is primarily concerned with future goals and change.

Notes for Chapter 1

1 Yukl & Gardner III (2020).
2 Northouse (2021).
3 French Jr. & Raven (1968).
4 Stogdill (1974).
5 Northouse (2021).
6 Mumford, Zaccaro, Harding, Jacobs, & Fleishman (2000).
7 Lewin, Lippit, & White (1939).
8 Stogdill (1969).
9 Bowers & Seashore (1966).
10 Blake, Mouton, & Bidwell (1962).
11 Hersey & Blanchard (1969).
12 Fiedler (1964).
13 Goleman, Boyatzis, & McKee (2013).
14 Drucker (1996).
15 Yukl & Gardner III (2020).
16 Graen & Uhl-Bien (1995).
17 DeRue & Ashford (2010).
18 Pfeffer & Salancik (2003).
19 Quigley & Hambrick (2015).
20 Pendleton & Furnham (2016).
21 Grint (2010).
22 Inspired by concepts in Grint (2010).
23 Rittel & Webber (1973).
24 Adapted from Karelaia & Van der Heyden (2020).
25 Northouse (2021).
26 Fayol (1949).
27 Drucker (1974).
28 Simonet & Tett (2013).
29 Pendleton & Furnham (2016).
30 Schein (2010).
31 Hackman (2010).
32 Rucci, Kirn, & Quinn (1998).

Know yourself: Leadership traits, skills, and behaviors

This chapter will enable you to:

» Recognize the importance of self-awareness as a key leadership skill.
» Examine the link between personality traits and effective leadership.
» Assess which problem-solving, human, and technical skills you will need to develop to perform well in a leadership role.
» Reflect on the impact of different leadership styles and behaviors on your effectiveness as a leader.

For a long time, leadership was viewed as a 'gift' that extraordinary people possessed more or less from the very beginning of their lives. Thus, it would be unlikely you could become a leader if you were not born that way. This 'leaders are born, not made' view has changed in recent decades, and nowadays it is accepted that **through learning, practice and determination, everyone can develop effective leadership skills**.

The first step to growing as a leader is to get to **know yourself**. Knowing yourself means identifying your current traits, skills, and behaviors as the starting point in your development path. If you are aware of your personal attributes, you will also know what your current strengths are, and what you need to improve to become a good leader.

Personality traits

Personality traits are **patterns of feeling, thinking and behaving that characterize each of us as individuals.** These traits are relatively stable throughout a person's life; they may change, but only in the long term.[1]

In the previous chapter we learned that personality does not necessarily have a direct influence on the effectiveness of an individual as a leader. However, being aware of your personality traits is important, because they can affect many aspects that are relevant in your leadership development, such as your motivation, the way you approach situations, or your attitudes in interpersonal relations.

Personality traits help to define our 'comfort zone' of behaviors that we find natural and easy to perform, because they are consistent with our individual attributes. Behaviors outside the comfort zone require more effort and practice, and we tend to find them more difficult to perform. Developing as a leader involves **recognizing your 'comfort zone' behaviors** that mesh with your personality, but also learning how to move into your zone of discomfort.

BUILD YOUR LEADERSHIP SKILLS

SOME ADVICE ON HOW TO
STEP OUT OF YOUR COMFORT ZONE

Here are some ideas that can be helpful when you want to exit your comfort zone:

- **Identify and visualize what is outside your comfort zone.** For example, by drawing a circle and putting inside it the things that you are comfortable with, and outside it the things that challenge you.
- **Learn to get comfortable outside your comfort zone through practice and small steps.** For example, if you are not comfortable with small talk, you can gradually bring this behavior into your comfort zone by practicing it (in the elevator, at the coffee machine, etc.).

- **Recognize and accept fear.** Acknowledge that you are afraid of certain situations and do not hide behind excuses. This will help you to focus on what is actually challenging you and improve your capacity to work on it.
- **Accept and value failure.** You will certainly fail or underperform when you start acting outside your comfort zone. Each failure or mistake must be taken as a learning opportunity and used to move one step forward.
- **Envision the benefits.** Recognize and keep in mind the benefits that will come from stepping out of your comfort zone, for example in terms of personal well-being and/or professional growth. This will increase your motivation and help you to overcome fear.

The most common way of categorizing personality is the '**Big Five**' **classification**, which identifies these five key dimensions of personality:[2]

- **Conscientiousness**: to what extent an individual is responsible, dependable, and organized.
- **Extraversion**: how much an individual is sociable, talkative, and outgoing.
- **Openness to experience**: how much an individual is open-minded, curious, and eager for new experiences.
- **Emotional stability**: to what extent an individual is able to remain stable and balanced in their emotions versus easily becoming anxious, angry, or insecure.
- **Agreeableness**: how much a person is likable, kind, flexible, and sympathetic.

Research has demonstrated that out of the 'Big Five' dimensions, **conscientiousness** is the one that has the strongest positive correlation to performance in work tasks.[3] Being linked to planning, organization, and consistency, conscientiousness can definitely support both a leader's development and the disciplined execution of certain tasks connected to leadership (although it is not universally related to leadership effectiveness).

This does not necessarily mean that you cannot become a good leader with limited conscientiousness. You will, however, probably need to step out of your 'comfort zone' when you have to practice those leadership skills that are regularly associated with conscientiousness (such as the ability to plan, persistence, task commitment, or reliability).

Extraversion facilitates interpersonal interaction and may allow someone to be recognized more quickly and easily as a leader in a social context. The more outgoing and assertive you are, the more other people will perceive that you can provide direction and guidance, which in turn may improve your effectiveness as a leader. Therefore, if you have an extraverted personality you may have an 'advantage' as a potential leader.[4]

However, research has also highlighted that introverts can make equally or even more effective leaders. As Susan Cain argues in her book *Quiet: The Power of Introverts in a World That Can't Stop Talking*, our contemporary societies tend to consider the extravert to be the 'ideal' type of person and have a rather negative perception of introverts. Cain and other researchers, however, demonstrate that **introverts can be very effective leaders too**.[5] Introverts tend to listen carefully to others and reflect thoroughly on situations. They get their energy and ideas from their inner world, which helps them to conceive of superior solutions. Moreover, pairing extraverted leaders with a group of proactive employees can potentially lead to interpersonal conflict, while the same group of employees would succeed if led by a more introverted person.[6]

Similar to extraversion, **openness to experience** can help performance in some instances, but not in others. Being open to new experiences facilitates leadership development and effectiveness, since it will increase your motivation to explore new paths and learn. Furthermore, openness to experience helps leaders to deal with different cultures and different perspectives in heterogeneous teams. Being open to experiences is also an asset in a fast-changing world and in an environment that poses new challenges on an almost daily basis.

At the same time, however, if you constantly want to explore new ways and easily get tired by the status quo, you might have a disadvantage in circumstances that require careful attention to existing norms and values.[7]

Emotional stability is related to leadership effectiveness because leaders often need to tolerate high levels of stress and frustration, for example when responding to pressures from the environment or aggression from others without overreacting. However, a certain degree of 'instability' in emotional reactions can be positive too, since it is associated with the ability to experience passion and enthusiasm, and the transfer of such feelings to followers.

Finally, and maybe surprisingly, **agreeableness** is the 'Big Five' trait that is least clearly associated with leadership.[8] Agreeableness is a desirable trait in social interactions, but it does not seem to lead to higher leadership effectiveness. Agreeableness could even be detrimental to your effectiveness as a leader when it lowers your ability to make tough final decisions and 'disappoint' people.

Although not universally linked to leadership, agreeableness has been shown to have a positive effect in certain circumstances or when interacting with other factors. For example, recent research shows that in situations where group cohesion and interdependence is very important (such as in collectivistic societies—cultures that value mutual dependence within groups), agreeableness is a strong predictor of leadership quality.[9]

It is important to note that low levels in a personality dimension that is positively correlated to leadership effectiveness can still lead to effective results, if the trait is in appropriate combination with other dimensions. For example, research has shown that leaders who are low on conscientiousness and high on extraversion, agreeableness, and emotional stability tend to stimulate higher job satisfaction and job commitment in their followers.[10]

Our discussion on the role of the 'Big Five' traits reveals some **key implications:**

- A **self-assessment of your personality traits** is always helpful in your leadership development journey, since it helps you understand what motivates you, your strengths and weaknesses, the way you relate to the world, and how your traits compare with those of other people you work with. This enhances your self-awareness, which is a key skill for leaders, as we will learn later in this chapter.
- Each personality dimension can have **different positive effects on leadership effectiveness** (see Table 2.1), based on the context, how they manifest in a person, and how they interact with other factors and personality dimensions.

- If you don't possess a specific trait that is valuable in certain circumstances, you can still be effective by **stepping out of your 'comfort zone.'**

Personality trait	High	Medium or low
Conscientiousness	Consistency and reliability	Risk tolerance and dynamism
Extraversion	More easily recognized as a leader, ability to engage with others	Thoughtfulness
Openness to experience	Innovativeness	Loyalty to norms and values
Emotional stability	Stress tolerance	Passion, enthusiasm
Agreeableness	Empathy, flexibility	Assertiveness, decisiveness

Table 2.1 'Big Five' personality dimensions and their positive contribution to leadership effectiveness[11]

EXERCISE

ASSESS YOUR OWN PERSONALITY TRAITS

The following steps can help you better understand your own personality:

1. Draw five horizontal lines for the 'Big Five' personality traits: conscientiousness, extraversion, openness to experience, emotional stability, and agreeableness. Add 'Low' and 'High' labels at each end of the lines.
2. Try to make a self-assessment of your personality traits. Make a mark on the line where you would place yourself on each of the 'Big Five' traits.
3. Search for a psychometric test of the 'Big Five' traits online and complete it (at the time of writing a free test is available at, for example, *https://openpsychometrics.org/tests/IPIP-BFFM/*).

4. Compare the test results with your prior self-assessment. Which similarities and differences do you notice? What have you learned about your personality traits?

DISCOVER YOUR PERSONALITY TYPE

In the 1920s, the psychologist Carl Jung developed a theory of personality types based on how we perceive and interpret information about the world. Building on Jung's work, Katharine Briggs together with her daughter Isabel Briggs Myers created a personality test that has been widely used in organizations around the world, the Myers-Briggs Type Indicator test. It identifies 16 personality types, and can help you discover your psychological preferences and how they differ from those of others (e.g. other members of your team).

The Myers-Briggs version of the test needs to be paid for, but there are also some free versions of Jung-related personality tests available online (at the time of writing e.g. at *https://www.onlinepersonalitytests. org/personality-test/infp/*).

Another widely used personality test is the DISC test (DISC stands for the four personality factors of dominance, influence, steadiness and conscientiousness), based on the work of psychologist William Moulton Marston. You can also find different versions of this test online, e.g. there is a free version at *https://openpsychometrics.org/tests/ODAT/*.

Use one of these tests to find out more about your own personality type, and compare your results with that of your colleagues or fellow students.

Leadership skills

Individual skills are a fundamental building block of good leadership. Unlike personality traits, which are considered more stable and difficult to change in the short to medium term, **skills can be learned, practiced, and developed.**

In the development of your leadership skills, there are three core areas that you need to focus on:[12]

- Problem-solving skills
- Human skills (intrapersonal and interpersonal)
- Technical skills

Problem-solving skills

It is vital for leaders to **develop problem-solving skills** because, as we have discussed in Chapter 1, one of the distinctive features of leadership is the ability to address very difficult ('wicked') problems.

Empirical research has identified some key problem-solving skills that you should work on in your leadership development path, namely:[13]

- The ability to **define problems** and **distinguish between symptoms and causes**
- The ability to **creatively generate possible solutions**
- The ability to **plan actions and predict** the possible consequences of the actions
- The ability to **implement a plan**, including **identifying alternative actions** if the plan does not work out as expected

The ability to **define problems** refers to being able to identify and correctly frame the actual problems affecting an organization, a group, or a social context.

Imagine, for example, that you are the coach of an amateur football team, and your team is underperforming, having lost many games in a row. The problem of poor performance could be defined in different ways. For example, it could be framed as a purely physical and 'technical' issue, in the sense that players have low technical skills or are in a poor athletic condition, or it could be framed as a problem that encompasses the motivation and self-confidence of the team.

The ability to define problems is important because it may allow you to **tease out a more fundamental problem from its 'symptoms.'** In our example, it may be that framing the problem as a purely technical one diverts your focus from the more fundamental problem, that is a lack of motivation and team spirit.

Carefully defining the problem also involves **breaking down the problem into smaller parts**, so that it is easier to **search for possible causes**.

For example, if the problem of your football team is framed as a motivational one, its various parts may be identified in aspects such as: a lack of individual self-confidence, lower enthusiasm and less fun experienced by the players, or a high frequency of interpersonal conflicts. The separate parts of the problem can then be related to possible causes. Here, these causes might be the fact that some well-respected players have left the team, or some players come from disappointing experiences in other teams, or there are lingering, unresolved relational issues among team members.

Once the causes of the problem have been identified, it is your task as a leader to set some clear goals that, once achieved, will enable you to overcome the problem. What are your short-term and medium- or long-term goals?

For example, one short-term goal could be to restore the team spirit by strengthening friendships and creating a sense of common purpose among the players. In the longer term, you could aim to improve team unity and cohesion during the matches. This would eventually lead to an improvement in the team's performance.

Once your causes and goals are clarified, the **ability to generate solutions** comes into play.

The ability to generate solutions involves exercising **creativity**. There are many techniques that are associated with the development of creativity. In your leadership development path, you will need to acquire some of these fundamental techniques, which involve both your own creativity and your ability to engage your followers in creative efforts.

The main **skills that are associated with creativity in leadership** are:

- **Imagination**: the ability to visualize ideal solutions (including apparently unrealistic ones)

- **Critical thinking**: the ability to challenge established assumptions and embrace different perspectives
- The ability to **listen to others and welcome alternative points of view**, promoting open discussions and brainstorming

CREATIVE PROBLEM SOLVING FOR LEADERS

In his book *Solve It! The Mindset and Tools of Smart Problem Solvers*, management professor Dietmar Sternad identifies five main phases of a systematic problem-solving process, which he succinctly summarizes in a '5Cs' model:[14]

1. **Clarify** (make sure to solve the right problem)—where you need the ability to define problems.
2. **Causes** (make the right diagnosis)—where you need the ability to distinguish between symptoms and problems.
3. **Create** (find promising solutions)—where you need the ability to creatively generate possible solutions.
4. **Choose** (decide on the optimal solution)—where you need the ability to plan and predict the possible consequences of your actions.
5. **Commit** (make it happen)—where you need the ability to implement your plan.

In the chapter on the 'Create' phase, Sternad summarizes a few methods that you can use to generate solutions and enhance your own creative problem-solving skills as well as your team's:

- **Question assumptions and constraints** (*"What if they weren't that important after all? And even if they might be, what could you do to overcome the constraints?"*).
- **Describe the problem in a more abstract way** and then **learn from other people** who have solved a similar problem before (*"Who has already found a way to handle such a problem?"*).

- **Use a smart form of brainstorming** (in which you first let people work on solutions individually, then discuss their ideas in small groups, and only then—and after a break—use group discussions).
- **Try reverse brainstorming** (asking *"How can we cause the problem?"* instead of *"How can we solve the problem?"*).
- **Use creativity techniques** like logic trees (a structured overview of all options for solving the problem), mind maps, or thought experiments (*"What would happen if…?"* or *"What would it look like if…?"*).

The **ability to plan and forecast** is crucial for implementing solutions. A key leadership ability here is to be able to anticipate and predict what exactly might happen when you start to execute your plans. You should be able to identify different potential scenarios, ranging from the best to the worst possible case.

In our football team example, you may not get the results you want in terms of improving team morale and cohesion, or in terms of performance outcomes. Thus, you need to be able to consider these potential negative outcomes, and have an idea of how you would deal with them.

In relation to this, you also need to take into account the **constraints**: those factors that influence and possibly limit the solution to the problem. In our example, improving performance by addressing low motivation in the team could be limited by the personality of some members, or by the difficulty of creating frequent and effective occasions to socialize, since the members of the team have many other commitments besides participating in team-related events. It might also be that the team's performance is limited by the talent of the players.

Finally, the **ability to implement the planned solutions** may involve the knowledge of basic **project management skills**, and this is more related to the technical-management aspect.

For a leader, implementing solutions effectively requires the **human skills** that we will analyze further in this chapter. It also requires being able to **address potential issues that might occur when executing the plan**. If your proposed solution leads to negative outcomes, what is your 'plan B'? Research suggests that effective organizational leaders are those who can quickly and flexibly find alternative ways to pursue their goals in the event of unexpected obstacles derailing their initial plans.[15]

Having one or more 'plan B's' does not imply you need to have a 'goal B,' where you decide to aim for a less desirable result. It means being able to recalculate your route toward reaching your goal. Having a 'plan B' increases your confidence as a leader in implementing your 'plan A,' since it gives you a psychological safety net. Having a 'plan B' also allows you to consider other solutions, and that could even lead to a more effective redefinition of the problem.

In our football example, a possible 'plan B' for restoring a climate of motivation and enthusiasm could be to replace some experienced players with junior players from the youth team.

SOLVE PROBLEMS LIKE ELON MUSK[16]

Elon Musk is a well-known entrepreneur and investor, founder and key leader of companies such as Tesla and Space X. Musk has highlighted several times that he uses an approach to problem solving called 'first principles,' which dates back to the Greek philosopher Aristotle. This approach asks you to analyze a problem starting from the most fundamental aspects and then build up your solution from those basics. More specifically, the application of first principles implies that you identify what is assumed to be true in relation to a given problem and then challenge every basic assumption.

Musk describes how Tesla (the automotive and clean-energy company he co-founded and led) solved the problem of the high cost of the battery packs used in electric automobiles. He started from the taken-for-granted 'truth' that 'battery packs are inevitably expensive and the cost will not decrease significantly in the future.' Historically, the cost was US$600 per kWh. Then he challenged this 'truth' by breaking down the problem into its fundamental (first) principles, asking himself: 'what are the material components of the batteries?'

Musk then considered how much these materials (such as nickel, cobalt and aluminum) separately cost on the spot market, for example on the London Metal Exchange.

And he found out that the fundamental problem was not the cost of each component material. The total cost of the components was approximately US$80 per kWh—much less than US$600. Instead, the actual problem was to find a 'clever' and economic way to assemble the components into a battery.

Applying the first principles approach allowed Elon Musk to focus on the 'actual' problem and consider the main constraints to resolving it. The solution involved creating a process that combines the components at a sufficiently large scale to reduce the cost. This led to the creation of Tesla Gigafactory, solely dedicated to the cost-efficient assembly of lithium-ion batteries.

Human skills

As a leader, you need to be constantly aware of the fundamental connection between problem-solving skills (that refer to cognitive abilities) and human skills (that are more related to relationships and emotions).

There are two basic categories of human skills: **personal skills** and **interpersonal skills**.

Regarding personal skills, the most important ones that you should consider in your leadership development are connected to **self-awareness**.

According to the organizational psychologist Tasha Eurich, self-awareness is the ability to recognize your own values, passions, and motivations, and to see how they fit with your environment and how they impact on others.[17]

Self-awareness is important for leadership because it helps you to build an attitude of **core self-evaluation**. Core self-evaluation is your own fundamental appraisal of your "worthiness, effectiveness, and capability as a person."[18] Research has consistently found that leaders with a high level of core self-evaluation are more capable of building confidence in followers and motivating them to achieve better results.[19]

Self-awareness thus helps you to develop a more accurate understanding of your strengths and increase your confidence in yourself (**self-confidence**) and in what you can do (**self-efficacy**). On the other hand, it also prevents you from the negative effects of having a level of core self-evaluation that is too high and unrealistic.

BUILD YOUR LEADERSHIP SKILLS

HOW TO BUILD YOUR SELF-AWARENESS

Here are some ideas for improving your self-awareness:

- Take **personality tests** to get to know yourself from various angles
- Ask for **honest feedback** from friends, colleagues and peers on your personality and general behaviors, as well as how you acted in specific circumstances
- **Listen openly** to the feedback you get, without justifying, arguing, or explaining
- **Keep a journal or write notes** reflecting on your own behaviors and thoughts
- Clearly **formulate your goals** and reflect on what ultimately motivates you
- **Identify your comfort zone** (see the box on pages 26–27)
- **Reflect on your actions and decisions**—for example, ask whether the outcomes of a decision are as you expected, or why things went in a certain way
- Rely on **professional support** (for example, work with a coach)

In addition to self-awareness and core self-evaluation, effective leadership also requires **interpersonal skills** that involve your **ability to understand people and social situations**.[20]

Research has identified some key interpersonal skills that are crucial for a leader. Those can be summarized as:[21]

- **Social intelligence**: the ability to understand other people's perspectives and goals in relation to different problems and solutions. In other words, this allows you as a leader to answer questions such as: What problems do others face? What is important to them? What motivates them? Social intelligence for a leader can be defined as "empathy applied to problem solving."[22]
- **Behavioral flexibility**: the ability to adjust your behaviors based on other people's point of view. This is linked to social intelligence and allows leaders to cope with changing situations that present new demands. It is important to highlight, however, that behavioral flexibility cannot be stretched too much. As organizational psychologists David Pendleton and Adrian Furnham warn, it is unlikely that a leader can master the entire repertoire of possible behaviors and attitudes to thrive in any situation.[23] As we will see later in Chapter 3, if you recognize that some issues require an approach that you are too uncomfortable to adopt, you may need to involve other people and/or delegate the task in a team-level effort.
- **Social performance** includes a range of different competences. The most important ones include being able to communicate your vision and perspective to others, being able to mediate in conflict situations, and being able to coach followers, providing them with guidance and support. In Chapter 5 we will explore a set of tools that can help you develop such competences.

The combination of personal and interpersonal skills can be summarized in an overarching skill that is increasingly important for today's leaders: **emotional intelligence**. It is defined as the ability to recognize, understand and manage your own emotions, as well as the emotions of those around you. The term was popularized by the psychologist Daniel Goleman, after being created by personality researchers John Mayer and Peter Salovey in 1990.[24]

Emotional intelligence is composed of the following three interconnected skills:

- **Empathy**: the ability to understand other people's emotions. It is constantly ranked at the top of the leadership skills required in contemporary organizations and society. Research shows that leaders who excel in empathy outperform in motivating, engaging, and coaching employees through major challenges.[25]
- **Self-regulation**: the ability to manage emotions and impulses in a way that is appropriate for the situation. This is seen, for example, in the ability to avoid outbursts and overreactions.
- **Emotional self-awareness**: self-awareness specifically applied to moods and emotions. Emotional self-awareness is concerned with understanding how emotions shift and change, and how they impact interpersonal relationships and the ability to carry out tasks.

ASSESS YOUR OWN LEVEL OF EMOTIONAL INTELLIGENCE

Decide how often the statements in the table below apply to yourself, choosing between A = 'Never,' B = 'Sometimes,' and C = 'Often.' Then allocate the points in the three results tables on the following page to get your emotional intelligence (EI) profile in the three dimensions of self-awareness, self-regulation, and empathy. For each dimension, 5–8 points would indicate a relatively low level of EI, 9–11 a medium level of EI, and 12–15 a high level of EI.

	Statement	A	B	C
1	I know which 'emotional triggers' cause strong negative feelings for me.	○	○	○
2	In discussions with other people, I deliberately try to see things from their perspective too.	○	○	○
3	I tend to have emotional outbursts when I am frustrated about something.	○	○	○
4	I am good at helping other people to feel better when they are feeling down.	○	○	○
5	I am fully aware of my emotions when I am experiencing them.	○	○	○
6	I can manage stress and anxiety very well.	○	○	○
7	Other people tell me that I am a good listener.	○	○	○
8	I am able to calm myself down quickly when something bad is happening to me.	○	○	○
9	It is difficult for me to express my feelings.	○	○	○
10	I become defensive when I am criticized by others.	○	○	○
11	Reading other people's emotions is quite difficult for me.	○	○	○
12	I am well aware of my main strengths and weaknesses.	○	○	○
13	I remain calm when facing a challenging situation.	○	○	○
14	I find it difficult to give critical feedback to other people in a way that does not trigger negative reactions from them.	○	○	○
15	I am aware how physical reactions in my body (e.g. butterflies in my stomach) are connected to my emotional state.	○	○	○

SELF-AWARENESS

Question	How to allocate points	Your points
1	A-1, B-2, C-3	
5	A-1, B-2, C-3	
9	A-3, B-2, C-1	
12	A-1, B-2, C-3	
15	A-1, B-2, C-3	
Total points (max. 15)		

SELF-REGULATION

Question	How to allocate points	Your points
3	A-3, B-2, C-1	
6	A-1, B-2, C-3	
8	A-1, B-2, C-3	
10	A-3, B-2, C-1	
13	A-1, B-2, C-3	
Total points (max. 15)		

EMPATHY

Question	How to allocate points	Your points
2	A-1, B-2, C-3	
4	A-1, B-2, C-3	
7	A-1, B-2, C-3	
11	A-3, B-2, C-1	
14	A-3, B-2, C-1	
Total points (max. 15)		

EMOTIONALLY INTELLIGENT LEADERSHIP FROM FACEBOOK COO SHERYL SANDBERG[26]

May 1, 2015 was a fateful day for Facebook COO Sheryl Sandberg. The family was celebrating her husband Dave Goldberg's 50th birthday when he unexpectedly passed away. Sandberg, who had always been used to being in charge and solving wicked problems, was suddenly faced with a completely new situation that was very difficult for her to cope with. In a Facebook post, she wrote about a choice that she now had to either "give in to the void, the emptiness that fills your heart, your lungs, constricts your ability to think or even breathe," or to find meaning in the hardship. Unfortunately, she wrote later on in the month following her husband's death that she "spent many of my moments lost in that void."

It was difficult for her to get back on track again. In a meeting on her first day back at work, she started rambling and then fell asleep. She was experiencing deep grief, just like millions of other people do.

But Sandberg didn't only understand and accept her own feelings (and even made them public—and herself vulnerable—with her widely shared Facebook post, and later in a book in which she described how she built resilience and found joy again after facing adversity). She also recognized that she wanted to help others who were going through a similarly difficult emotional phase in their own lives.

In February 2017, Sandberg announced that Facebook would considerably extend bereavement leave "to give our employees more time to grieve and recover," as well as "paid family leave so they can care for sick family members as well." Facebook employees would now get up to 20 days of paid bereavement leave for an immediate family member and up to six weeks of paid leave when they need to care for a relative who has fallen ill.

Thus, in addition to emotional self-awareness and the ability to express and manage her own emotions, Sandberg also showed a high degree of empathy, understanding what such an exceptional emotional state means for others. She also took concrete action that showed how much she cared about the emotional well-being of her team.

Technical skills

Unlike problem-solving and human skills, **technical skills** are hard to generalize as they depend on the specific context where you operate as a leader.

Technical skills include **specialized knowledge about methods, processes, and tools** for conducting the work tasks you are responsible for as a leader.

For example, within a manufacturing company, technical skills include knowledge about the company's products and production processes, and general knowledge about the organization's structure, systems, and assets.

Technical skills are acquired through different paths that involve formal education, on-the-job training, and experience.

In an organization, the importance of technical skills (relative to problem-solving and human skills) typically changes according to the position that leaders occupy in the management hierarchy, i.e. if their responsibility is at a top management, middle management, or operational supervision level.

While all three types of skills are generally important across all levels, typically, technical skills are more important at the operational supervision level, whereas generic problem-solving skills may be relatively less crucial. On the other hand, technical skills are less crucial at the top management level, where instead the ability to solve complex (and 'wicked') problems becomes more important. For middle managers, the three groups of skills are usually of equal importance.

This helps to explain why successful CEOs are often 'generalists,' meaning that they can move across industries which may be technically very different. They are still able to achieve successful outcomes in very different contexts, because their talent lies mostly in the human and problem-solving skills that are required in their positions.

On the other hand, you cannot expect to lead effectively without a good level of context-specific technical knowledge. Research clearly shows that **leaders with technical skills gain higher levels of trust and recognition** from their followers and are better able to foster team performance.[27]

Thus, even if the technical expertise that is required in your leadership position is not part of your formal education, you should put effort into acquiring it as quickly as you can, at least to a basic level. Use the opportunities that the context offers you to engage in on-the-job learning!

Behavioral styles

There are two fundamental aspects of **leadership behavior** that you need to consider in your leadership development:

- The relative importance that you place on **people** versus the **task at hand**
- Your attitude toward **decision making**

People- versus task-orientation

Are you more task-oriented (focusing on what matters to get things done), people-oriented (you want the people you work with to be happy), or some combination of the two?

A common framework that can be used to map your orientation in the people versus task space is the **Leadership Grid**, developed by social psychologists Robert Blake and Jane Mouton.[28] This framework identifies five leadership styles based on the combinations of high/low people-orientation and high/low task-orientation.

The styles along with their main features are shown in Figure 2.1.

Figure 2.1 Leadership styles based on task- and people-orientation[29]

Be aware that although the 'team leadership style' appears as the ideal combination at first sight, there may be situations that require more focus on one dimension than the other. For example, if you are introducing a big change to the workplace that impacts people's habits and feelings, it could be preferable to place a higher emphasis on people than on productivity. On the other hand, if your company is facing economic difficulties and its survival is at risk, you will probably need to focus on achieving higher levels of efficiency and productivity in the short term.

The self-assessment exercise below can help you to understand whether you are more people- or task-oriented, so you can gain a better idea of how you operate as a leader and identify ways that you can improve your ability to consider people or the task depending on what the situation needs.

ASSESS YOUR OWN LEADERSHIP STYLE

Decide whether you mainly agree or disagree with the 16 statements in the table below. When you have finished answering, count the number of 'A' answers as indicated on the following page to find out whether you are more people-oriented or task-oriented.

	Statement	A	B
		I mainly agree	I mainly disagree
1	I am a highly goal-oriented person.	○	○
2	Maintaining a positive work climate is more important than meeting every deadline.	○	○
3	I am good at breaking down complex problems into smaller tasks that can more easily be accomplished.	○	○
4	I love to coach other people so that they can develop their full potential.	○	○
5	It is easy for me to manage my time and priorities well.	○	○
6	The most important job of a leader is to achieve goals.	○	○
7	The most important job of a leader is to create trust (between the leader and the team as well as between team members).	○	○
8	It is important to give everyone in my team a voice in the decision-making process.	○	○
9	I thrive when I can work on challenging tasks.	○	○
10	I am used to meeting all of my deadlines and demand the same of others whom I work with.	○	○
11	I want everyone who works with me to be happy.	○	○
12	It is a leader's job to focus on the satisfaction and well-being of their team members.	○	○
13	I very much want to maintain a good relationship with everyone in my team.	○	○
14	I usually take a very structured approach to problem solving.	○	○
15	I have excellent planning and organizing skills.	○	○
16	It is important to ensure that everyone feels valued in a team.	○	○

Decision making

Making effective decisions is a core task for a leader.

Using Kurt Lewin's model as a basis, you can reflect on your preferences and attitudes toward decision making as a leader.[30]

There are three major **decision-making styles** that you could adopt as a leader (see also Figure 2.2):

- **Autocratic style,** where you make decisions without consulting the members of your team. This may be because the decisions do not normally require input from the team and/or the consensus of the team is not important for implementing the decisions. The autocratic style has the advantage of being highly efficient as it can enable quick decision making, and is therefore particularly effective in highly dynamic situations or during crises. However, the autocratic style can create a climate that may be demotivating for the team members.

- **Democratic (or participative) style,** where you are responsible for making the final decisions, but you involve team members extensively in the decision-making process, for example in the generation of possible solutions, in gathering information about the context of the decision, or in evaluating alternative courses of action. The democratic style encourages creativity and engagement, and therefore creates higher individual satisfaction among the members of the team. However, when quick decisions are needed, the democratic style may be ineffective or counterproductive.

- **Laissez-faire style,** where the responsibility to make decisions is largely delegated to the team members who, as a consequence, have high autonomy in how they organize their work. As a laissez-faire leader, you can provide support and advice if requested, but you otherwise don't get involved. This freedom can lead to high job satisfaction among team members, but it can also be inappropriate in teams where people have low skill levels, little motivation, or poor knowledge.

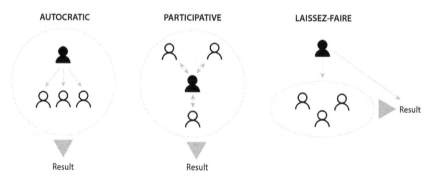

Figure 2.2 Lewin's decision-making styles

As we will see in Chapter 3, the efficacy of the different styles, and the need to adjust your approach to decision making, mainly depends on the characteristics of the followers.

EXERCISE

DETERMINE YOUR DECISION-MAKING STYLE

Indicate to what extent you agree or disagree with the statements in the table below. When you have finished answering, count up your points according to the instructions below the table to identify your preferred decision-making style.

	Statement	I fully agree	I some-what agree	I do not agree
1	When people understand the goals of the organization and their role within it, you just need to let them do their work to get good results.	2 points	1 point	0 points
2	Supervision and control are important aspects of a manager's job.	2 points	1 point	0 points
3	As a leader, I am the one who is always responsible for making decisions.	2 points	1 point	0 points
4	I have a lot of trust in other people in general, and in the people with whom I work in particular.	2 points	1 point	0 points
5	Tasks need to be clearly assigned and controlled in order to ensure the successful completion of an important project.	2 points	1 point	0 points
6	Everyone in the team should get a chance to be heard before making an important decision.	2 points	1 point	0 points
7	Micromanaging is the wrong approach. Most people are capable of making good decisions and understanding what is important in their work on their own.	2 points	1 point	0 points
8	I am happy giving orders to others.	2 points	1 point	0 points

Statement		I fully agree	I some-what agree	I do not agree
9	I like to brainstorm ideas with others in order to identify the best solution to a problem.	2 points	1 point	0 points
10	When I work in a team setting, I try to encourage everyone to participate.	2 points	1 point	0 points
11	I am happy to let other team members make decisions on behalf of our team.	2 points	1 point	0 points
12	I usually consult with others when I need to make a difficult decision.	2 points	1 point	0 points
13	It is important that everyone in an organization follows procedures correctly.	2 points	1 point	0 points
14	Leaders can give general direction and support, but it is not their job to give detailed instructions about how to do things.	2 points	1 point	0 points
15	Teams works best when they collectively make decisions.	2 points	1 point	0 points

DETERMINE YOUR DECISION-MAKING STYLE

Decision-making style	How to calculate it	Insert your total points per style here (on a scale of 0–10)
Autocratic style	Add up your points for questions 2, 3, 5, 8, 13	
Democratic (participative) style	Add up your points for questions 6, 9, 10, 12, 15	
Laissez-faire style	Add up your points for questions 1, 4, 7, 11, 14	

WARREN BUFFETT—A HIGHLY SUCCESSFUL LAISSEZ-FAIRE LEADER

Warren Buffett is widely considered to be one of the most successful investors in the world. As chairman and CEO of Berkshire Hathaway, he has developed the company from a mid-sized textile manufacturing firm into one of the largest and most valuable corporations in the world.

When Buffett buys a new company (which he has done considerably more often than most people), he does not interfere with the day-to-day business of it. Instead, he fully focuses on getting the best possible managers into his team—people who, as he said, he would "like and admire," and who then run the company for him.[31] There are three characteristics that he is looking for, in particular, when hiring people: "integrity, intelligence and energy."[32]

He then gives his managers just three rules to follow: to run the business (a) as if it was 100 percent owned by them, (b) as if it was the only asset they (and their families) would ever possess, and (c) as if it could never be sold or merged for at least 100 years.[33] Other than that, he tries to create an "environment of freedom"[34] in which the managers can take their own decisions about all aspects of their business.

The high degree of autonomy also enables Buffett to maintain a head office that seems rather tiny compared to other corporations of a similar size, with barely more than two dozen employees.[35]

Buffett once compared his leadership style to managing a golf team: "If Jack Nicklaus or Arnold Palmer were willing to play for me," he said, "neither of them would get a lot of directives from me about how to swing."[36]

Surrounding himself with highly motivated and capable people, making sure that they understand the long-term values of his corporation, and then putting them fully in charge of running the business—this 'hands-off' (laissez-faire) leadership approach has served Warren Buffett very well on his way to becoming one of the richest and most widely admired businesspeople in the world.

KNOW YOURSELF—LEADERSHIP TRAITS, SKILLS, AND BEHAVIOR: A BRIEF SUMMARY IN 10 POINTS

1. The first step to growing as a leader is to get to **know yourself**, by identifying your current traits, skills, and behaviors as the starting point in your development path.

2. **Personality traits** are patterns of feeling, thinking, and behaving that characterize each of us as individuals. They don't directly determine your effectiveness as a leader, but define your basic attitudes and your 'comfort zone.'

3. The most common classification of personality traits is the '**Big Five**': conscientiousness, extraversion, openness to experience, emotional stability, and agreeableness.

4. **Leadership skills** include problem-solving skills, human skills, and technical skills.

5. **Problem-solving skills** involve your ability to define problems, generate solutions, and plan and implement actions.

6. **Human skills** have a personal and interpersonal facet. The key aspects at the **personal level** are self-awareness and core self-evaluation. The key aspects at the **interpersonal level** are social intelligence, behavioral flexibility, and social performance.

7. Personal and interpersonal human skills can be summarized in the core skill of **emotional intelligence**.

8. **Technical skills** include specialized knowledge about methods, processes, and tools related to the tasks that you are responsible for as a leader.

9. **Behavioral styles** refer to your preferences as a leader in how you deal with people and how you rely on people to make decisions.

10. In addition to **task-orientated versus people-orientated behavioral styles**, we can distinguish between **autocratic, participative or laissez-faire (delegative) decision-making styles**.

Notes for Chapter 2

1 Roberts & DelVecchio (2000).
2 Costa & McCrae (1999).
3 Witt, Burke, Barrick, & Mount (2002).
4 Judge, Bono, Ilies, & Gerhardt (2002).
5 Cain (2012).
6 Grant, Gino, & Hofmann (2011).
7 Nahavandi (2009).
8 Judge, Bono, Ilies, & Gerhardt (2002).
9 Javalagi & Newman (2021).
10 Smith & Canger (2004).
11 Inspired by concepts in Kaiser, LeBreton, & Hogan (2015).
12 Katz (1974).
13 Mumford & Connelly (1991); Zaccaro, Mumford, Connelly, Marks, & Gilbert (2000).
14 Sternad (2021a).
15 Mullins & Komisar (2009).
16 Adapted from Dyer, Furr, & Lefrandt, C. (2019).
17 Eurich (2018).
18 Judge, Erez, Bono, & Thoresen (2003).
19 For example: Resick, Whitman, Weingarden, & Hiller (2009).
20 Zaccaro, Mumford, Connelly, Marks, & Gilbert (2000).
21 Northouse (2022); Zaccaro (2001).
22 Northouse (2022).
23 Pendleton & Furnham (2016).
24 Salovey & Mayer (1990).
25 Development Dimensions International, Inc. (2016).
26 Based on information in Luscombe (n.d.); Sandberg & Grant (2017); Sandberg, Matloff Goler, & McGee (2017).
27 For example: Van Minh, Badir, Quang, & Afsar (2017).
28 Blake, Mouton, & Bidwell (1962).
29 Inspired by contents in Blake, Mouton, & Bidwell (1962); Blake & Mouton (1978).
30 Lewin, Lippitt, & White (1939).
31 Cunningham (2014), p. 54.
32 Buffett (1998).
33 Cunningham (2014), p. 55
34 Ibid., p. 56.
35 Elkins (2017).
36 Cunningham (2014), p. 53.

How to lead (with) others

- -

This chapter will enable you to:

» Recognize how different followers may respond better to different types of leadership behavior.
» Examine how the relationship between you and your followers influences your effectiveness in the leadership role.
» Explore how you can help your team members develop, learn and grow with a transformational leadership approach.
» Identify the key aspects that determine your team's performance.
» Evaluate the benefits and risks of a shared leadership approach.

- -

The **characteristics of your followers** and the **interactions between you and your followers** are essential aspects that you need to consider in order to improve your leadership effectiveness.

As we learned in Chapter 1, followers are a vital asset in any leadership situation. Without followers, there is no leadership, and healthy leadership is a shared effort between leaders and followers toward the attainment of common goals.

To **build a good leader–follower relationship**, you should consider these aspects:

- The **followers' characteristics** (for example in terms of their competences, motivation, maturity, or experience) that influence the most appropriate behavior (style) to adopt, in accordance with the goal that needs to be accomplished.

- The **relationship between leader and followers**; this relationship evolves over time and should be, as much as possible, aimed at pursuing personal growth and development goals.
- The **team context**, since leaders and followers typically interact in a team setting. In some cases, it may even be that the leadership itself is exercised within and through a team, where leaders and followers may exchange their roles or have both roles simultaneously.

The characteristics of followers

In Chapter 2, we discussed how leadership behavior can be composed of different styles (task- versus people-oriented; and autocratic, participative, or laissez-faire).

There is no 'one best way' here, i.e. one style that is superior to the other(s). Instead, each style or combination of styles can be more (or less) appropriate depending on the needs of a specific situation.

Research (mostly within the situational and path–goal approaches to leadership) has shown that the **leadership requirements in different situations depend mostly on the characteristics of the followers,**[1] especially:

- their competence and skills to perform a given task, and
- their motivation and commitment toward the accomplishment of a given task.

These characteristics can be positioned in a 2x2 matrix that identifies the most appropriate leadership style for each situation (see Figure 3.1).

When followers have **low competences and skills,** for example because they are new to a certain activity or task, and **low motivation and commitment,** in the sense that they are not really driven to put effort into accomplishing their goal, then it would be appropriate to adopt a **'Direct and monitor'** style of leadership (*Quadrant II*).

We can consider this style to be a combination of task-oriented and autocratic behavior, in the sense that you give followers detailed and precise instructions on what goals need to be achieved, and on how to go about accomplishing them. Then you carefully supervise your followers. During this supervision process you should try to adopt an open attitude that is aimed at increasing your followers' commitment, so that (if possible) the situation moves toward *Quadrant III*.

In *Quadrant III*, followers still have **low competences and skills**, but **high levels of motivation and commitment**. In this situation it is preferable to adopt a '**Coach and instruct**' style, which means that you still provide detailed instructions to your followers on how exactly to accomplish the goal, but at the same time you leverage their motivation to encourage them to learn and improve in the required skills. You can do so, for example, by asking them for input and involving them in discussions about the activity. This style can be seen as a combination of people-oriented and autocratic.

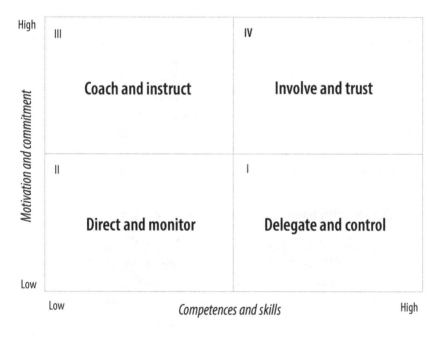

Figure 3.1 Followers' characteristics and leader's behavior (The 'how to lead' matrix)

Quadrant I is the opposite: you have followers with **high competences and skills** but **low levels of motivation and commitment**. In this case, you can leverage the abilities of your followers and assign them tasks that they know how to accomplish very well. However, given their low motivation, you need to be careful to make sure these tasks are actually completed. This usually means constantly following up on the goals. Therefore, the recommended leadership style is '**Delegate and control**,' which can also be seen as a mix of the laissez-faire and task-oriented styles.

Finally, in *Quadrant IV*, you have followers that have both **high competences and skills** as well **high motivation and commitment**. In this situation, you can rely on your followers knowing how to accomplish a task. Therefore, you don't need to give them detailed instructions and directions. At the same time, you can trust your followers have the motivation needed to pursue their goals, so there is no need to control them, because the high motivation acts as a 'self-control' mechanism.

The leadership style that is most appropriate here is '**Involve and trust**.' It can be seen as a mix of people-oriented and democratic styles, or alternatively, as a mix of people-oriented and laissez-faire styles. In working toward attaining the goals, you may need to actively involve the motivated and skilled followers in joint decision making (people-oriented and democratic), or, when needed, leave them complete freedom to act and decide by themselves (people-oriented and laissez-faire).

Just as important as the characteristics of your followers is the type of relationship that you as a leader establish with your followers. Let us therefore take a closer look at this crucial aspect of leadership.

The relationship between leader and followers

A very straightforward way to look at the leader–followers relationship is with the **contingency model of leadership**. It was developed by the industrial psychologist Fred E. Fiedler in the 1960s.[2]

This model suggests that there are three relevant aspects of the leader–followers relationship:

- The **'good' versus 'bad' relationship** that you have with your followers, based on the degree of mutual respect, trust and confidence.
- The **high versus low power** that you can have over your followers, based on the formal position that you have (for example, based on whether you have the capacity to give rewards or 'punishments' to your followers).

- The **high versus low degree of task structure**, which refers to the clarity of the task that needs to be performed. A highly structured task is characterized by clear procedures and is easy to control. On the other hand, a task with low structure is unclear and ambiguous.

These dimensions identify situations where a task-oriented style is more appropriate than a people-oriented style (and vice versa).[3]

If your **relationship with your followers is good**, you are in a **strong formal position of power**, and the degree of **task structure is high**, you are encouraged to adopt a **task-oriented style**. In this case, you don't need to focus on building relationships or improving trust, confidence and mutual respect. You can fully concentrate on accomplishing your goals.

Let us imagine, for example, that you are leading a team with the task of completing a project. The team likes and respects you (so your leader–follower relationships are good). You're in a management position of strength, as you have been formally appointed to lead the team on this project, and you know exactly what to do in the face of a structured task. In this situation, a task-focused leadership style would be most effective.

However, if you are in a **weak position of power** and/or the **task structure is low**, even if your relationships with your followers are good, it is generally preferable to adopt a **people-oriented style** in order to preserve the good relationships and trust, which could potentially be damaged if you adopt a style that is too 'production-oriented' without having sufficient formal authority. The people-oriented style will also allow you to collect ideas and suggestions that can help in an unstructured situation.

If you are in a **strong formal position of power**, but you have **poor relationships with your followers and/or the task structure is low,** it is again appropriate to adopt a **people-oriented style**, because your first focus should lie in improving your relationships with the group in order to 'justify' your formal position.

Imagine, for example, that you have a new job in a new company, and you are replacing a leader who has just retired and was highly popular, respected and admired by the team. The team probably views you with skepticism and may not trust you to the same extent. We can therefore say that you have a poor relationship with your followers. On the other hand, your formal power is high because you're officially in charge of the team. You can assign the tasks, plan the work, evaluate performance, and give rewards and penalties. In this situation, it is better to act as a people-oriented leader, that is a leader who can focus on building relationships first.

If you have **poor relationships with your followers,** and you are also in a **weak formal position of power** and the **task structure is low,** it is best to strengthen your position by setting clear rules on how to get the job done. Thus, a **task-oriented approach** is preferable. This may sound counter-intuitive, but the rationale behind this is that adopting a people-oriented style in the face of an ambiguous task, with low trust from your followers and low formal power as a leader, will increase the likelihood of conflicts and tensions, resulting in indecisiveness and paralysis of the group.

EXERCISE

REFLECT ON THE FACTORS THAT AFFECT YOUR LEADERSHIP EFFECTIVENESS[4]

Think of a situation where you have been in a leadership role (either formal or informal), where you have needed to accomplish a specific task by leading your followers. Answer the following questions:

1. How effectively were you able to accomplish the task? How would you rate your own performance and your team's performance in accomplishing the task?
2. How would you evaluate the competences and abilities of your followers in relation to the task?
3. How would you describe your relationship with your followers? Was it mainly positive, or was it tense and conflictual?
4. What was the degree of task structure? Were there clear goals, or were the goals ambiguous? Were there clear rules and few paths to take, or many paths with unclear directions?

5. How would you rate your own competences and abilities in relation to the task?
6. How would you describe your formal power in this situation? Did you have some 'official' authority? Could you give rewards or penalties to followers? Were you in charge of assigning tasks?
7. How would you describe the leadership style that you mostly adopted in this situation? Is it more people-oriented or task-oriented? Is it mainly directive, participative, or delegative?

After answering these questions, use the models described in this section (The 'How to lead' matrix in Figure 3.1 and the Fiedler model) to identify and assess the fit between your leadership style and your followers' characteristics, your relationship with them, and the task itself. How does this fit (or misfit) impact on your leadership effectiveness?

The dynamic view of the leader–followers relationship

The relationship between you and your followers is **not a static one**. As a leader, you interact on a daily basis with your followers, thus building **a relationship that evolves over time**.

We also need to consider that the leader–follower relationship develops on an individual basis. Each one-to-one relationship (also called a 'dyadic' relationship) has its specific characteristics and is defined in terms of the **quality of the social exchange**. The quality of a relationship can be assessed in terms of the benefits and costs that each participant experiences from the social interaction.

The **leader–member exchange (LMX) model** helps you to reflect on the different types of relationships that you may develop with your followers and on the consequences of these social exchanges varying in quality.[5]

Research has demonstrated that a person holding a leadership role has the tendency to differentiate followers into two groups (see also Figure 3.2):

1. the **in-group**, which is the 'inner circle' of the followers' team and is characterized by high-quality exchanges with the leader, and

2. the **out-group**, which comprises the followers who are not part of the leader's inner circle and who have lower-quality relationships with the leader.

OUT-GROUP

- Lower quality exchange
- Weaker collaboration
- Low trust and disengagement

IN-GROUP

- Higher quality exchange
- Strong collaboration
- High trust and engagement

Figure 3.2 The in-group and out-group according to leader–member exchange (LMX) theory

The high-quality relationships between the leader and the in-group members have many positive features, for example high mutual respect, high reciprocal trust, and the provision of opportunities for professional growth and development.

Followers in the in-group get more support from their leader. Their contributions are valued and recognized, sometimes even beyond what is 'fair' and 'objective.' Similarly, mistakes or errors made by in-group followers might be overlooked by the leader or judged with benevolence.

These positive attitudes create a favorable context for the performance of the in-group followers, who feel the desire to compensate the leader for their in-group status. Therefore, they will work hard, behave in loyal and supportive ways, take on tasks that are not formally required, and display a high commitment to the goals set by the leader.

In contrast, the **team members that are in the out-group** have a lower-quality relationship with the leader, which is characterized by less frequent or absent interactions and fewer opportunities for development. They are also perceived by the leader as having lower abilities, competences, and motivation, are usually assigned to more 'ordinary' tasks, and are sometimes subject to blame even beyond their responsibilities.

As a result, the out-group followers experience more stress and discrimination, which ultimately leads to job performance deterioration, which in turn strengthens the 'out-group feeling.' As a consequence, out-group members are more likely to become disloyal to their leader and to the organization, and engage in disruptive behaviors.

EXERCISE

WHAT IT MEANS TO BE PART OF THE IN-GROUP OR OUT-GROUP

Think about a social situation where you, as a team member, have experienced an in-group/out group separation (for example, among fellow students or friends, or in a work context).

- Were/are you in the in-group or the out-group?
- What were/are your feelings associated with your status as an in-group or out-group member?
- How did/do you see people in the 'other' group?

When you have a leadership role, it is almost natural that you develop a closer (high-quality) relationship with a sub-group of followers, for example because you know them well from previous experiences, or because you have a better rapport, or because you rely on their key competences and specialist support.

This is generally a positive development; it can help you a lot in accomplishing your leadership tasks. It can also help to mitigate the stress and pressure that are associated with your role.

However, you should prevent this high reliance on loyal and close contacts from developing into an **in-group/out-group situation with possible detrimental effects**, such as:

- **The risk that out-group members develop apathy or hostility toward the team**. As a consequence of the stress and discrimination they experience, out-group members are more likely to become disloyal and engage in disruptive behaviors.[6]

- The **risk that you and the in-group members become overly confident**, disregard input and criticism from elsewhere, and become less creative, innovative, and effective in problem solving. This phenomenon is well known to social psychologists under the label of 'groupthink.'[7]

These risks can be mitigated by:

- Periodically reflecting on the preferences that you may have toward some followers, and considering if these preferences may bias your judgement and create feelings of discrimination. This can be aided simply by talking one-to-one to the team members who may experience more 'out-group' feelings.
- Helping out-group members to feel involved and empowered, for example through using the in-group followers as ambassadors for building and maintaining interpersonal relationships.
- Considering different in-group/out-group combinations for different activities, identifying tasks where the competences of out-group members can be particularly valuable.
- Providing development and training opportunities where you or other members of the in-group act as coaches or mentors.
- Actively asking out-group members for their opinion and advice on important matters.

CASE STUDY

HOW IN-GROUP OVERCONFIDENCE GROUNDED AN AIRLINE[8]

Swissair used to be the pride of Switzerland—a widely admired airline with a global network and a seemingly unrivalled reputation for quality and financial strength (it was even commonly known as the 'flying bank').

In the early 1990s, Swissair's management decided to embark on an aggressive expansion strategy with the aim of becoming one of the major players in the European airline business. But a promising merger project with three other European airlines from Austria, Scandinavia, and the Netherlands failed in 1993 (with insiders claiming that Swissair's management had negotiated too arrogantly).

With the help of the management consultancy firm McKinsey & Company, Swissair then developed its 'Hunter' strategy as a new attempt to grow quickly through acquisitions. Swissair bought shares of different airlines "of dubious quality," and paid over 5 billion Swiss francs for the acquisitions (instead of the 0.3 billion francs originally budgeted for the expansion program).

During the expansion phase, the CEO hardly faced any resistance from a homogeneous and cohesive in-group in the board of directors, which the leading Swiss newspaper NZZ described as "a body packed with [political party] grandees who still spoke Swiss German at their meetings."

By 2001, it was clear that the expansion strategy, which had remained uncontested for a long time, had ultimately failed. The corporate structures had become too complex to manage, and the company had stretched itself far beyond its financial capabilities. The CEO and the board resigned, Swissair went bankrupt, and the final Swissair flight touched down at Zurich airport.

Several experts and commentators considered the phenomenon of groupthink as one of the key factors that contributed to the hubris and demise of Swissair. Overconfidence, the belief of being invulnerable, and an organizational set-up that discouraged dissenting opinions based on an overly strong in-group became a toxic cocktail.

Leader-member exchange and the newly appointed leader

The social exchange view of leadership is particularly important for a **leader who is new in the role.**

As highlighted by leadership researchers Susan Ashford and Scott DeRue, a leader's authority is not ensured by simply holding a formal position.[9] Instead, the role of the leader, and the corresponding role of the followers, is built through a **social interaction process which is made up of 'claims' and 'grants' by the people involved.**

In general, claims are made by the person that wants to be identified and recognized as the leader, whereas grants are given by the people that agree to be followers. Claims and grants can be statements, but also behaviors, acts, and non-verbal cues.

The development of a leader–follower relationship is a sequence of claims and grants. It can have a self-reinforcing or self-defeating progression (see Figure 3.3).

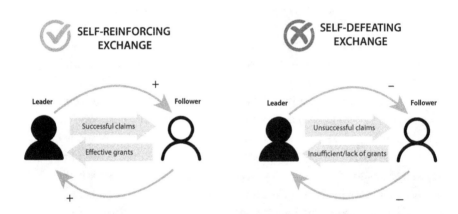

Figure 3.3 Self-reinforcing and self-defeating exchange dynamics in leader–follower relationships

Imagine, for example, that you are a newly appointed young coach of a sports team. You meet the players for the first time, replacing an unsuccessful coach. You address the team by telling them: "I am here to revolutionize our style of playing this year." This is a clear claim that potentially puts you in a strong leadership position (as someone who is bringing disruptive change and expecting the team to follow).

The team members can 'grant' their followership by saying, "Yes! We need it!" Then you can explain your ideas in more detail, thus starting a progression of claims and grants that reinforce your early leadership.

But it could also be the case that the team members (or at least some of them) do not immediately grant you your 'revolutionary leader' role. For example, one experienced player may look skeptical and say, "We tried every revolution in the past and nothing worked out."

What you are expected to do now is to reply with a further claim. There are different ways to do this.

You could oppose the skeptical player in an assertive way, for example by replying, "I am sure that your teammates have a different opinion." This could initiate a 'granting' dynamic from other members of the team that disagree with their fellow player. But it could also initiate a 'deterioration spiral' whereby other players follow their teammate and undermine your leadership by intensifying a confrontational attitude.

Your claim in reply to the skeptical player could, however, be more open and constructive. You could say, "Then let's explore the reasons why everything hasn't worked so far!" This may possibly bring the 'claiming/granting' exchange back on a positive track.

This example shows the importance of some key aspects in the leader–follower exchange, which are especially relevant if you are a newly appointed leader, or if you want to be regarded as a leader in a situation where you don't have a legitimate position of power:

- **Leadership does not necessarily come from holding a formal position.** It is possible that although you are formally appointed as a leader, followers do not recognize your leadership.
- On the other hand, a **group can recognize the leadership of someone who is not formally identified as a leader.**
- Thus, **leadership is constructed and continuously reconstructed** through the leader's exchanges with their followers (in an ongoing 'claiming/granting' process).
- Claiming and granting can be a **mutually reinforcing process** that strengthens the leader's and followers' roles, or a 'downward spiral' that undermines the leader–follower relationship.

The transformational power of the leader-follower relationship

The most effective leaders are the ones that are able to orient the exchange with their followers toward continuous learning, improvement, and growth.

This feature is a core characteristic of a **transformational leader.**[10] James MacGregor Burns, who first introduced the concept of transformational leadership, defined it as a process where "leaders and their followers raise one another to higher levels of motivation and morality."[11]

But what does it mean specifically to be a transformational leader, and what should you work on to enhance the transformational dimensions in your leadership development?

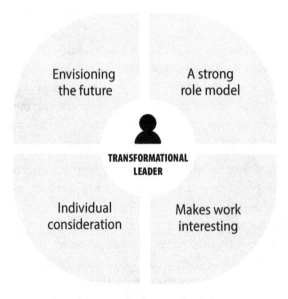

Figure 3.4 Key features of a transformational leader

These are the key features of a transformational leader according to the first and most established conceptualization by leadership scholars Bernard M. Bass and Bruce J. Avolio (see also Figure 3.4):[12]

- Transformational leaders are **strong role models**. Being a role model implies that you can exercise **idealized influence** on your followers. Idealized influence is a set of behaviors that increase the followers' identification with the leader, such as: setting an example of dedication and hard work, sacrificing self-interest or personal gain to benefit the followers and/or the organization, and demonstrating that you mean what you say by doing it yourself and following through.

- Transformational leaders **care about each one of their followers** in a distinctive way. This means that as a transformational leader, you need to have **individualized consideration** for the people you work with. This includes, for example, understanding preferences on work tasks and individual strengths and weaknesses, but also being open to discussing personal motivations, ambitions, struggles and dreams, and being able to provide encouragement and support when needed.
- Transformational leaders create and communicate **a positive and engaging vision of the future**. If you provide a compelling vision to your followers, you create a climate of **inspirational motivation**, where the group works together for a greater aim. This will increase the intrinsic motivation of the followers because the everyday work tasks will assume a new meaning related to the vision and the associated values and ideals.
- Transformational leaders **make the work interesting**. As a transformational leader, you need to offer **intellectual stimulation** to followers, for example by assigning challenging work tasks that allow them to learn and grow. You should as far as possible encourage your followers to get out of their comfort zone, and challenge them with problems that stimulate imagination, creativity, and the development of original solutions.

Other refinements and elaborations on the idea of transformational leadership may offer further insights for your personal development.

James Kouzes and Barry Posner, for example, identify **five practices that transformational leaders adopt** when interacting with their followers:[13]

1. **Modeling the way**: developing clear guiding principles and sticking to them
2. **Inspiring a shared vision**: elaborating a common vision to channel the energies of the followers

3. **Challenging the process**: taking initiative and risks by supporting good ideas that change the status quo
4. **Enabling others to act**: creating situations where individuals are empowered to act and succeed
5. **Encouraging the heart**: acknowledging the contributions of followers and celebrating their achievements

You can also use various approaches that focus on deepening specific aspects of transformational leadership.

For example, the concept of **visionary leadership** highlights the transformational ability to envision the future in an inspirational and engaging way, and is a helpful model to refer to when you are dealing with change and innovation in organizations and social contexts.[14]

Other perspectives suggest that to be a transformational leader, you don't necessarily need to always be 'under the spotlight', constantly displaying your charisma and influence. On the contrary, the concern for followers' growth and the focus on the greater good encourage effective leaders to adopt styles including '**servant leadership**'[15] or '**invisible leadership**'[16]

IDENTIFY THE CHARACTERISTICS OF TRANSFORMATIONAL LEADERS

Below is a list of leaders that are commonly portrayed as 'transformational.' Choose two or three of them and research their leadership characteristics. Then identify for each person which transformational leadership characteristics are particularly visible and which ones are less visible. Do they have any 'controversial' characteristics that may even, in your view, bring their status as a 'transformational' leader into question?

- Jacinda Ardern (politician)
- Mary Barra (businessperson, CEO)
- Bill Belichick (American football coach)
- Napoléon Bonaparte (emperor)
- Jeff Bezos (businessperson, founder and CEO)
- Winston Churchill (politician)
- Walt Disney (businessperson, founder and CEO)
- Mahatma Gandhi (politician, thought leader, philosopher)
- Steve Jobs (businessperson, founder and CEO)
- Martin Luther King (civil rights activist)
- Jack Ma (businessperson, founder and CEO)
- Nelson Mandela (politician)
- Angela Merkel (politician)
- Jean Monnet (politician)
- José Mourinho (soccer coach)
- Elon Musk (businessperson, founder and CEO)
- Indra Nooyi (businessperson, CEO)
- Barack Obama (politician)
- Michelle Obama (former lawyer and first lady)
- Adriano Olivetti (businessperson, founder and CEO)
- Mother Teresa (nun and missionary)
- Jack Welch (businessperson, CEO)
- Oprah Winfrey (talk show star, television producer)

DO YOU HAVE THE POTENTIAL TO BECOME A TRANSFORMATIONAL LEADER?

Indicate whether you mainly agree or disagree with the statements in the table below.

	Statement	A I mainly agree	B I mainly disagree
1	I find it easy to create trusting relationships with other people.	◯	◯
2	I try to give my best in everything I do, and I demand the same of others whom I work with as well.	◯	◯
3	I often give constructive and critical feedback to other people (who highly value it).	◯	◯
4	I am good at helping others find meaning in their work.	◯	◯
5	I know exactly what my values are, and I often talk about them with others.	◯	◯
6	People usually feel inspired when I tell them what we could achieve together.	◯	◯
7	I am always confident in my interactions with other people.	◯	◯
8	It is easy for me to recognize and understand the needs of other people.	◯	◯
9	Other people often tell me how much they value my encouragement and support.	◯	◯
10	I am very concerned about the well-being of the people I work with.	◯	◯
11	In a teamwork situation, I usually do more work than other team members actually expect of me.	◯	◯
12	I am good at identifying the strengths and weaknesses of other people, and understanding their values.	◯	◯
13	When solving a problem, I like to listen to and consider other opinions, even if they wildly differ from my own.	◯	◯
14	It is important that I consider the ethical or moral consequences of the decisions that I make.	◯	◯
15	Other people come to me for advice and appreciate being coached by me.	◯	◯
16	I consider myself to be a self-confident, decisive, and determined person.	◯	◯

Now count the number of your 'A' answers. The more 'A' answers you have, the higher your potential to be a transformational leader.

Leading teams

The interactions between leaders and followers very often take place in a team context. A **team** is a small group that has a defined common purpose, and whose members have interdependent roles, as well as complementary skills.[17] Examples of teams in the business context are project teams, new product development teams, self-managed work teams, management teams, and top executive teams.

It is important to consider the team dimension because it requires some additional reflection on the leadership–followership process that goes beyond the dyadic view that we have discussed above.

In particular, as a leader, you need to focus on the following **key aspects that determine your team's performance:**[18]

- Clarity of roles and coordination
- Assessment and development of members' skills
- Group cohesion, cooperation, and trust
- External alignment

Let us now take a closer look at each of these aspects.

Clarity of roles and coordination

As a leader, you should clearly **explain the responsibilities** assigned to each team member and highlight the relevant procedures and routines that may need to be followed to perform specific tasks. This will be the first step in improving **team coordination**, which is a crucial aspect in performance.

The leader's influence on team-level performance has specific challenges because it does not only depend on the motivation and skills of individual members (which can be managed in the dyadic relationship), but also on how followers mutually coordinate to use their skills and focus their efforts to achieve the common goal.

Performance in a team depends on the mutual coherence and synchronization of the activities of the team members. As a leader, you can promote better coordination by carefully **planning roles and activities** before work on a task starts.

Coordination is achieved not only by planning in advance, but also through making **mutual adjustments during the course of the task**. For example, in a basketball game, a big part of the team's performance depends on their ability to execute the strategies that they agreed upon with their coach, but another big part depends on the reciprocal observation of and reaction to each other's moves and actions during the game. This continual coordination is facilitated by members' skills, joint experiences, and culture.

Assessment and development of members' skills

As a leader, it is your responsibility to regularly **assess the skills of your followers** with the aim of identifying gaps and requirements for upskilling.

You are expected to fulfill this task by giving **constructive feedback** and sometimes directly **coaching** your team members (see also Chapter 5). Alternatively, you can delegate coaching activities, mentoring, and giving feedback to more experienced team members, especially if the activities concern new or junior members.

Another way to develop the skills of your team members can be to plan formal courses, workshops, or other training activities.

Group cohesiveness, cooperation, and trust

If you lead a highly **cohesive team**, it is more likely that you can obtain the best from their joint performance, because there is a higher sense of identification with the common purpose. This can enhance motivation and promote extra-role effort.

To enhance cohesion, you should constantly highlight the presence of shared objectives and mutual interests, and clearly illustrate how cooperation helps the team to reach their objectives.

Mutual trust and cooperation in a team can be improved by:

- Elaborating and communicating a **vision** of what the team can achieve through effective cooperation
- Using **ceremonies, symbols, and rituals** to make team membership appear as something special and unique

- Organizing **team building activities** and planning social events outside of work
- **Informing the team about achievements** related to their performance
- Constantly **reviewing the 'health status' of your team's climate and relationships** by involving all the members in joint self-assessment sessions

You also need to be aware that teams that are too cohesive run the risk of developing groupthink, which, as we have seen above, is dangerous for team performance and even survival. This risk needs to be monitored through periodic self-reflections and 'reality checks.'

JÜRGEN KLOPP'S TEAM LEADERSHIP STYLE[19]

Jürgen Klopp has the reputation of being one of the world's best soccer coaches. After several stunning successes with teams in his home country of Germany, he's been credited with being the mastermind behind ending Liverpool FC's three-decades-long trophy drought as he led the 'Reds' to the English Premier League title in 2020, just over a year after winning the Champions League, Europe's most prestigious cup title.

Klopp is widely considered to be a role model for transformational leadership, with his ability to bring out the very best of his team. Here is a short summary of some of the key elements of his leadership style:

- **Have a clear vision and set challenging goals.** When Klopp arrived in Liverpool in 2015, he promised to "win the title" within four years (it turned out be five years in the end, but that didn't matter too much to Liverpool fans). At the same time, he clearly envisioned how he wanted the team to achieve this goal. He expected everyone to play "very emotional, very fast" and "at full throttle," and to "take it to the limit in every single game."

- **Develop strong personal connections.** "I like my players and let them feel it," said Klopp in an interview with *Impulse* magazine, adding that he always thinks about how others would like to be treated so that they can "work with joy and be totally committed to perform." Klopp is known for showing genuine interest in and care for the people he works with (and for giving them a hug from time to time).
- **Create a positive team spirit.** It was clear from the beginning for Klopp that he wanted to change not only the way in which the team played, but also the team spirit "from doubters to believers," as he called it. He strongly focuses the team on what they can achieve together, and on creating a 'can-do' attitude, in which "you have to at least see the chance that it can work out," even if things are not yet perfect.
- **Always give your best.** Klopp is widely known for showing his emotions and passions. "I give everything," he once said, and he would always expect the same of his team members (which is perfectly aligned with Liverpool FC's motto "intensity is our identity"). Everyone can feel how much Klopp cares, and this positive spirit has indeed become contagious.

External alignment

If your team operates in a broader organizational context (for example as a new product development team in a manufacturing company), you also need to ensure that its tasks and goals are consistent with other activities in the **internal organizational context** and in the **relationships with external stakeholders** whose decisions have an impact on the team (for example, clients).

External alignment is crucial for obtaining resources and support for the team's activities. Such resources include, for example, funds, materials, facilities and equipment, but also help from powerful actors inside and outside the organization.

Examples of **how external alignment can be achieved and strengthened** are:

- Maintaining an efficient and effective flow of communication with key actors within the internal and external contexts
- Nurturing a network of contacts who can provide relevant information (and encouraging followers to do the same)
- Consulting with other units and departments in the organization, and monitoring the progress of their activities where it affects the team's work
- Interacting with clients and external stakeholders

Shared leadership in teams

Teams may increase their effectiveness when the leadership role is not held by a single individual but, instead, is shared among the members.

Shared leadership emerges when team members instigate a dynamic and interactive influence process in which they lead one another to the achievement of common goals.[20]

If you promote shared leadership, you don't expect to be in a dominant position as the appointed leader, but rather you support the idea that you and your followers mutually influence each other and collectively fulfill leadership roles, tasks, and responsibilities.

Shared leadership can take different forms. Researchers and practitioners also use different labels to refer to this phenomenon and its various manifestations, for example, **distributed leadership, co-leadership, joint leadership, or collective leadership**.[21]

This sharing of leadership functions can be found in many high-tech start-up companies, where there is a rough division of labor in the leadership in the form of role specialization among the founders.[22] For example, a start-up management team comprising a tech expert, a sales specialist, and a generalist manager could lead the company in such a way that each one leads the team in relation to the tasks that are consistent with their expertise and competences.

Some of the **benefits of adopting a shared leadership approach** are:

- Higher levels of individual participation and collaboration, as team members feel more involved in impactful decisions

- The choices that are made are 'collectively owned,' and the team as a whole shares accountability for the decisions
- Members learn from one another and feel empowered to leverage their abilities
- Each individual leader feels less pressure and benefits from the professional and moral support of their co-leaders

Shared leadership can, however, be quite difficult in reality. If not implemented correctly, it can create serious problems for the functioning and performance of the team. For example, a major issue is **dealing with the established assumption that leadership is singular**. People tend to feel inspired and supported by a single specific leader. If this character is missing, people may experience a loss of engagement and motivation. Other problems may arise from the need for **consensus and mutual acceptance** in decision making that is central in shared leadership. Several forces make this harder: **competing personalities, different career goals**, and **personal agendas** might paralyze the shared leadership model.

The benefits and challenges of shared leadership emphasize the core message of this chapter, namely that leadership relies on the quality of social relationships.

SHARED LEADERSHIP PRINCIPLES AT HUAWEI: THE ROTATING CHAIRMAN SYSTEM[23]

The Chinese technology corporation Huawei was founded by Ren Zhengfei in the late 1980s. It soon expanded its business from manufacturing phone switches to a broad range of telecommunication equipment and consumer electronics. By 2022, it was a leading player in the global telecommunications industry, operating with around 195,000 employees and over 3 billion customers in over 170 different countries.

From the beginning, Zhengfei, who has been described as a leader with a "reflective and self-criticizing attitude," has always emphasized innovation in all forms and at all levels of the company.

In addition to technological innovation, Zhengfei also initiated a management innovation: he introduced a rotating CEO system at Huawei, in which three 'rotating chairs' each serve as a CEO for six months, supported by the same board of directors as a way to secure some degree of stability in the governance system. During their short tenure, the rotating CEOs are holding the highest leadership responsibility in the corporation. At the same time, Zhengfei has also kept his own (co-) CEO role, with a strong focus on coaching and mentoring the rotating CEOs.

"The company's fate cannot be tied to any single individual," is how Huawei officially comments on the system. "This collective leadership model is created upon common values, focused responsibility, democratic centralized authority, checks and balances, and growth by self-reflection."

HOW TO LEAD (WITH) OTHERS:
A BRIEF SUMMARY IN 10 POINTS

1. The **effectiveness of different leadership styles depends mostly on the situation**, which in turn is influenced by the characteristics of the followers.

2. The most important **characteristics of the followers** that impact on the situational effectiveness of leadership are their competences/skills and their motivation/commitment.

3. The combination of these characteristics identifies four situations (summarized in the '**How to lead**' matrix) where these different leadership styles are recommended: direct and monitor, coach and instruct, involve and trust, and delegate and control.

4. The **relationship between leader and followers** is crucial in determining the effectiveness of a more task-oriented versus a more people-oriented leadership style.

5. The quality of the leader–follower relationship is **dynamic**. It changes over time according to a process of **social exchange**, described by the leader–member exchange (LMX) model.

6. The **LMX model** helps you to reflect on the different relationships that you have with **in-group and out-group followers**, and recommends minimizing friction between in-group and out-group members.

7. The **social exchange view** is a useful perspective if you are a newly appointed leader and you need to gain respect and authority through a claiming and granting exchange 'game.'

8. **Transformational leaders** are able to orient the leader–followers exchange toward learning, improvement, and personal growth. Transformational leaders exert idealized influence on their followers, have individualized consideration, provide an engaging vision, and intellectually stimulate followers.

9. Most of the time, the leader–follower relationship takes place in a **team setting**. Key aspects that you must consider as a leader to **increase team effectiveness** are: clarity of roles, development of followers' skills, group cohesion, and external alignment.

10. A team could be characterized by **shared/collective leadership** rather than vertical/individual leadership. Shared leadership has many benefits but is difficult to implement.

Notes for Chapter 3

1   Hersey & Blanchard (1969); House (1996).
2   Fiedler (1964).
3   In Fiedler's model, task- and people-oriented styles are defined on the basis of a specific scale named the 'least preferred coworker' (LPC) scale, which synthesizes how much a leader has a 'human relations orientation' or 'task orientation.'
4   Inspired by a self-assessment exercise reported in Nahavandi (2012).
5   Graen & Uhl-Bien (1995).
6   Townsend, Phillips, & Elkins (2000).
7   Janis (1982).
8   Based on information in Hermann & Gulzar Rammal (2010); Tribelhorn (2021).
9   DeRue & Ashford (2010).
10 Bass & Avolio (1994); Burns (1978).
11 Burns (1978).
12 Bass & Avolio (1994).
13 Kouzes & Posner (2007).
14 Van Knippenberg & Stam (2014). On the role of visionary leadership applied to change, see also Chapter 4 in this book.
15 Greenleaf (1998).
16 Hickman & Sorenson (2013).
17 Yukl & Gardner III (2020).
18 Yukl & Gardner III (2020); Northouse (2021).
19 Based on information in Pearce (2019); Sternad (2020); Impulse magazine (2010), theguardian.com (2015).
20 Pearce, Conger, & Locke (2007).
21 Denis, Langley, & Sergi (2012).
22 Pittino, Visintin, & Compagno (2018).
23 Based on information in De Cremer and Tao (2015); Huawei.com (2022).

Contemporary leadership challenges

This chapter will enable you to:

» Reflect on the specific requirements of leading global and virtual teams.
» Recognize the importance of creating a strong ethical compass as a leader.
» Identify the main leadership competences related to creating more sustainable and inclusive organizations and societies.
» Confidently plan and lead change processes in both relatively stable and highly dynamic environments.

Regardless of the level at which you exercise your leadership role within an organization or in society, you will face constant challenges in a world that is increasingly complex, interconnected, and subject to rapid, unpredictable, and radical change.

These challenges involve three main areas:

- **Globalization**: physical trade between countries has been slowing down in recent years, suffering from planetary crises and shocks (e.g. the COVID-19 pandemic or armed conflicts). On the other hand, digital connectivity has increased exponentially, strongly affecting the globalization of labor markets and work relationships, and posing significant new challenges for leaders. **Virtual team leadership** skills are becoming more and more important, thanks to the increasing amount of remote collaboration across countries.

- **Ethics**: being a good leader implies that you behave with honesty and integrity, but also that you are aware of societal values that influence your relationship with followers and other stakeholders, and that you act in light of this. **Sustainability** and **inclusion** are among the values that demand the highest attention in contemporary society.
- **Turbulent change**: the pace of change has been accelerating constantly over the past 40 years. More recently, however, the nature of change has become more sudden and unpredictable. Leaders therefore need to work now more than ever on strengthening their **organizations' and team members' abilities to cope with change** and to be flexible and proactive.

In this chapter, we will take a closer look at these challenges and how you can respond to them as a leader.

Develop a global mindset and virtual leadership skills

Leaders are increasingly expected to act in a work environment that is characterized by ongoing interactions in physically remote settings and with distant cultures. This situation is no longer limited to big multinational enterprises, but is also becoming the reality for small firms and organizations.

This trend is fueled by the evolution and diffusion of platforms and applications that facilitate exchanges and connections on a global scale, at a lower cost and with higher accessibility.

The COVID-19 pandemic has accelerated this trend. At the same time, it has also amplified the need to address critical aspects of global collaboration, such as cultural and linguistic differences as well as spatial and temporal dispersion.

Leading across cultures

In a leadership role, you are expected to act in **social contexts**, where culture plays an extremely important role.

Culture is made of the values, norms, and customs that are shared by a social group. It guides the behavior of those groups, acting as a sort of "collective software" of people's minds.[1]

Effective leadership has different meanings in different cultures, and this applies especially when we consider culture at the level of nations as social groups. For example, the participative and egalitarian approach that is expected from a leader in Sweden would be less effective in China. Or an unstructured leadership approach, which is considered normal in Latin America and the Middle East, would be problematic in Germany.

As a leader, you need to be aware that **expectations regarding your role change according to the cultural context** in which you operate. You will need to modulate your behaviors in both individual and team relationships involving followers from different cultures.

Research has identified various ways to understand and work with different national cultures in global organizational settings.

For example, the social psychologist **Geert Hofstede** developed one of the most popular models for assessing **cultural dimensions** in a global context.[2] The basic model identifies five dimensions that differ across national cultures, namely:

- **Individualism**: how much individuals or small networks of close ties lie at the foundation of the social system (as opposed to **collectivism**, in which the needs of the group tend to take precedence over the needs and interests of individuals)
- **Power distance**: to what extent people accept an unequal distribution of power in society
- **Uncertainty avoidance**: how much ambiguity and uncertainty are tolerated in society
- **Masculinity**: how much value is assigned to assertiveness and competition in society
- **Time orientation**: to what extent people are oriented toward future and long-term goals

Other prominent examples are the cultural dimensions model of Fons Trompenaars and Charles Hampden-Turner, and Edward T. Hall's cultural factors model.[3] (There isn't room to go into detail about these models here, but if you are interested in learning more, there are weblinks that will take you to more information about them on the companion website of this book at *www.econcise.com/ConciseLeadershipTextbook*.)

REFLECTING ON YOUR OWN INTERCULTURAL EXPERIENCES

Think about your experiences of interacting with people from different cultures. Focus in particular on the following points and write down your reflections:

- **Verbal communication** (e.g. were there differences in how open people were to asking and/or answering personal questions?)
- **Non-verbal communication** (e.g. were there differences in how people viewed their 'personal space,' or in how physical touch and gestures were used? Were there differences in how people displayed their emotions?)
- **Collaboration** (e.g. were there differences in whether it was acceptable to speak out and frankly express opinions? Did people have different approaches to timing?)

A useful and comprehensive model you can refer to for learning about and reflecting on cross-cultural leadership is the **GLOBE model** (GLOBE stands for 'Global Leadership and Organizational Behavior Effectiveness'). Building on Hofstede's findings and combining them with other insights from cross-cultural management research, a group of scholars from 62 countries proposed a framework that comprises nine cultural values:[4]

- **Power distance**: the extent to which an unequal distribution of power is accepted
- **Uncertainty avoidance**: the importance of norms and rules to reduce unpredictability
- **Humane orientation**: whether fairness, generosity, kindness, and caring are valued
- **In-group collectivism**: the identification of individuals with their close networks (e.g. within a family or organization)

- **Institutional collectivism**: the identification of individuals with a broader societal interest
- **Assertiveness**: the prevalence of confrontational attitudes within groups
- **Gender egalitarianism**: the degree to which a society tries to minimize differences between men and women
- **Future orientation**: the emphasis on the future over the present or past
- **Performance orientation**: the focus on encouraging and rewarding performance

Based on differences in these nine values, the researchers identified different clusters of countries. These clusters map to six leadership styles that define what is considered most important in leader–follower relationships in the different cultures:[5]

- **Charismatic/value-based leadership**: with an emphasis on the ability to inspire and motivate on the basis on strong core values
- **Team-oriented leadership**: team building and common goals among members are important features of this leadership style
- **Participative leadership**: involving others in decision making and implementation is considered crucial
- **Humane-oriented leadership**: the leader is expected to be supportive, compassionate, and generous
- **Autonomous leadership**: individualism and independence are admired and appreciated in the leader
- **Self-protective leadership**: the leader is expected to ensure security for themselves and for the group, for example by 'saving face' or consolidating status

Table 4.1 gives an overview of which leadership styles are typically preferred in which clusters of countries.

Leadership style	Cultures where this style is valued the most
Charismatic/value-based	Latin America (e.g. Argentina, Mexico), Northern Europe (e.g. Sweden), South Asia (e.g. India, Thailand), Germanic Europe (e.g. Germany, The Netherlands), Anglo (e.g. USA, UK, Australia)
Team-oriented	Latin America, Confucian Asia (e.g. China, Japan), South Asia
Participative	Nordic Europe, Anglo, Germanic Europe
Humane-oriented	Anglo, Sub-Sahara Africa (e.g. Zambia, Nigeria), South Asia
Autonomous	Eastern Europe (e.g. Hungary, Poland), Germanic Europe
Self-protective	Eastern Europe, Middle East (e.g. Kuwait, Qatar)

Table 4.1 Preferred leadership styles across cultures according to the GLOBE research[6]

The insights from the GLOBE project provide a starting point for approaching the challenge of leading across cultures. It can help you to understand what your followers may expect from you, how to motivate them, and how to relate to them more generally. You can find out more about the GLOBE project at *www.globeproject.com*.

EXERCISE

YOUR CULTURAL MINDSET AND CULTURAL INTELLIGENCE

To succeed as a leader in a global environment, you need to develop a cultural mindset.[7] Holding a cultural mindset means you are able to take culture and cultural differences into consideration in your decisions, actions, and interactions with others. Cultural intelligence is a key component of a cultural mindset.

As a starting point, you can quickly test your cultural intelligence with the help of the following table. Indicate whether you mainly agree or disagree with the statements.

	Statement	A I mainly agree	B I mainly disagree
1	I find it easy to adapt myself to other cultures.	◯	◯
2	I know a lot about other cultures and religious beliefs.	◯	◯
3	I enjoy interacting with people from cultural backgrounds that are different from my own.	◯	◯
4	I have a lot of friends from other cultures.	◯	◯
5	It is easy for me to alter my communication style (including my non-verbal behavior) when I meet people from other cultures.	◯	◯
6	When meeting people from other cultures, I can quickly sense whether some form of communication or behavior is culturally appropriate or not.	◯	◯
7	I often try to get into conversations with people from other cultures.	◯	◯
8	I consciously apply my cultural knowledge when I interact with people from other cultures.	◯	◯
9	I am confident in dealing with unfamiliar situations when I meet people from other cultures.	◯	◯
10	Before I meet people from other cultures, I consciously think about how to best communicate with them.	◯	◯
	Number of 'A' and 'B' answers		

The more 'A' answers you gave (the maximum is 10), the higher your current level of cultural intelligence.

Leading virtual teams

Global leadership across cultures is increasingly being combined with the spatial and temporal dispersion of teams. Thus, knowing how to **lead virtual teams** has become a crucial requirement for leaders.

Researchers observed that leadership in a remote and virtual setting poses **additional challenges compared to 'on-site' leadership**.[8] For example, it is harder to form bonds and trust among team members and create a genuine dialogue in a virtual team. Moreover, it is easier for misunderstandings and conflicts to emerge and for team members to become disengaged.

Problems also arise when the geographical dispersion of the team is very wide, leading to a limited overlap in working hours. This causes a lack of direct communication, which may create a sense of isolation among individual team members.[9]

Figure 4.1 Leading a virtual team

If you are leading a virtual team, you should be aware of these issues and consider the following **practical guidelines**, based on both researchers' and practitioners' expertise (see also Figure 4.1):[10]

- **Schedule meetings as frequently as you can.** This is a way to compensate for the lack of both formal and informal interaction that members would otherwise have in a physical office. Be considerate of time zone differences by identifying suitable time slots that make a good compromise (e.g. avoid meetings where the same members always have to dial in late at night by introducing rotation, or identify times that are good enough for all members, such as early morning for Europe and late afternoon for Oceania). This can be facilitated by creating clear guidelines based on members' individual needs.

- **Keep everyone constantly informed.** In this way, all team members feel involved and are well prepared to participate in team efforts even if there is no synchronous virtual meeting in place. This can be further improved if you rely on a project management system or platform that manages each team member's tasks, and at the same time makes progress on the milestones continuously visible to everyone. This will also increase the sense of shared leadership across the team (see Chapter 3), benefitting the effectiveness of the joint work.

- **Establish an individual connection with team members.** As we saw in Chapter 3, it is important (particularly under the constraints of a virtual setting) to foster high-quality relationships with followers. Through virtual one-to-one connections, you can provide your followers with an opportunity to express individual concerns in a private interpersonal space, and this also gives you as a leader the chance to appreciate individual performance and show care for your team members. This can compensate at least partly for the absence of informal one-to-one conversations that happen in a physical office space, and for the increased difficulty in getting individual feedback (which in physical meetings can be gathered simply by looking at body language cues, such as people nodding, making eye contact, or showing engagement through their posture). Always keep in mind that the virtual space is much 'flatter' and less rich than physical reality.

- **Reduce the length of meetings and have frequent screen breaks** (or 'leg stretchers'—5 minutes every 40 to 45 minutes is usually enough). Be aware that attention spans are usually lower compared to an in-person meeting. Having shorter (and maybe more frequent) meetings will help you ensure that your team stays engaged.

- **Keep in mind the virtual setting when you are communicating.** For example, you need to pay attention to your gestures. When you are at a meeting table, large gestures can be effective, but on screen it may be more effective to limit your gestures and keep them closer to your body and within the frame of the camera. At the same time, it may be useful to distance yourself a bit from the camera, so that you don't appear as a 'talking head.' Showing more of your body increases your impression of trustworthiness, also when you listen to others.[11]

- **Set ground rules for virtual meetings.** Simple examples include asking participants to join in some minutes early (so that everyone can solve minor connection issues and check that their audio and video work properly), asking members to mute their microphones until they want to speak (this limits the distractions and 'surprises' from background noise), asking everyone to speak one at a time, or recommending members limit multitasking and stay focused on the meeting itself (which is again easier to implement in shorter meetings).

WHY LEADING VIRTUAL TEAMS CAN BE PHYSICALLY CHALLENGING: THE PHENOMENON OF 'ZOOM FATIGUE'[12]

Stanford Professor Jeremy Bailenson analyzed the impact of spending hours in videoconference meetings on the psychological state of office workers. He came to the conclusion that video chats lead to fatigue. Bailenson identified four main causes of what he called 'Zoom fatigue,' named after the popular videoconferencing software:

- Constant, intense eye-contact at a close distance, which can cause discomfort, especially when interacting with strangers.
- A high degree of cognitive load, where you constantly need to monitor the verbal and non-verbal behavior of other people, consciously attend to the effect of your own gestures, and keep technical aspects of the communication in mind too.

- Seeing yourself in the mirror all of the time. This leads to constant self-evaluation, which can be very stressful.
- Reduced mobility, as you cannot move around in front of the camera as much as you can in personal or phone conversations.

There are several ways of dealing with Zoom fatigue, including, for example, using external cameras and keyboards that increase your distance a bit, hiding the video of yourself to switch off the 'mirror,' or turning the video function off from time to time to give yourself a brief rest.

Construct and use your ethical compass for sustainability and inclusion

In the previous chapters, we've learned that as a leader you can have a real positive or negative influence on other people, and this implies a big ethical responsibility.

Ethics in leadership refers to the system of rules and principles that guide your decision making and behavior, by defining what is 'right' or 'wrong' and 'good' or 'bad.' This can be more precisely expressed in the following principles that are critical for defining the scope of ethical leadership:[13]

- **Honesty.** As an honest leader, you should refrain from any attempt to misrepresent reality or lie for your own interests. If you don't project honesty in your behaviors, you won't be seen as trustworthy and dependable.
- **Justice and fairness.** You should try as much as possible to treat your followers equally and provide everyone the same opportunities to participate, contribute, and receive fair rewards and recognition.
- **Respect.** You should have a sense of your followers' worth, and value them as individuals.
- **Community.** You should be altruistic in encouraging your followers' development rather than just being focused on your own per-

sonal success, for example by engaging in coaching, mentoring, and empowering behaviors.

- **Integrity.** You need to develop a strong moral purpose and be consistently true to it in your decisions and behaviors.

As you can imagine, adhering to these principles is not always easy. For example, you may face situations where being completely honest or following principles of fairness may lead you to violate other ethical obligations that you feel toward your team, such as when you are forced to lay off or sanction individuals, or disrupt the sense of community within your team.

These situations where there is an inherent contradiction in the application of ethical principles are called **ethical dilemmas**. As a leader, you face an ethical dilemma every time you need to make a decision in which each of the alternative courses of action that you could follow would require you to violate an ethical principle that you value.

EXERCISE

HAVE YOU EVER FACED AN ETHICAL DILEMMA?

Here are some examples of potentially contradictory ethical principles in a work context:

- Telling the truth
- Taking responsibility for your actions
- Following company policies
- Adhering to the norms of the profession
- Respecting commitments
- Following the law
- Acting in the best interests of the company's owners
- Acting in the best interests of the company's clients
- Refraining from causing harm to others
- Treating people equally

- Conducting sustainable business practices
- Pursuing valuable business opportunities

Taking the list above as inspiration, think about a situation (in a work context, as a student, or in any other social context) where you had to make a decision in which all the options available to you were in contradiction with at least one ethical principle that was important to you. How did you approach the issue? How did you arrive at a decision? What consequences followed your decision?

It is difficult to formulate a universal rule for solving ethical dilemmas (otherwise they wouldn't be dilemmas). However, as a leader, you can pay attention to some guidelines that will improve your approach to those dilemmas and increase your ability to take the 'right' path:

- **Identify in advance potential situations that are likely to trigger ethical dilemmas.** For example, decisions around hiring, firing, promoting, or rewarding followers. Recognizing ethical dilemmas in advance can help you to be more prepared.
- **Carefully prepare your response.** Visualize different scenarios than can emerge in dealing with ethical dilemmas and think about how you could respond and behave in each possible scenario. This 'rehearsal' is helpful because in emergency situations, you may have less time to respond, so you can refer to your repository of possible responses. Consider the following example: what would you do if you knew that your company was going to heavily downsize, and this would affect your team, but you were legally not allowed to forewarn them about this? This type of exercise can help you to imagine your feelings and inner struggles so they do not emerge as entirely new to you when you are actually faced with such a situation.
- **Assess all the information.** If you have time, consider carefully all the evidence that is available about the issue you need to make a decision on. Try to look at it from different points of view. Take the opportunity to consult with and get advice from trusted peers, mentors, or experienced colleagues.

- **Be courageous.** Be ready to experience painful and uncomfortable feelings after making a decision, even if you know that you have made the right choice. For example, if you find one of your most loyal team members has committed a serious violation, it may be difficult to decide to report them, but you must trust that you did the right thing in your role as a leader.
- **Reevaluate your decision before you act.** Take a different perspective on it. For example, think about how you would feel if you were one of the people affected by your decision, or how it would you feel if your decision was made public to everyone.

EXERCISE

WHAT IS YOUR LEADERSHIP STYLE IN ADDRESSING ETHICAL DILEMMAS?

There are different approaches that you can take to resolving ethical dilemmas. A questionnaire created by the researchers Michael C. Chikeleze and Walter R. Baehrend Jr. can help you to discover your prevailing attitude in addressing dilemmas (according to what they call different 'ethical decision making styles'). At the time of writing, the questionnaire is available online at *www.leaderdecisionmakingsurvey.com*.

The possible styles are classified as follows:[14]

- Duty-driven (*"doing what is right"*)
- Utilitarian (*"doing what benefits most people"*)
- Virtue-based (*"doing what a 'good person' would do"*)
- Care-oriented (*"doing what shows care to people that are close to me"*)
- Egoistic (*"doing what is personally beneficial"*)
- Justice-driven (*"doing what is fair"*)

To summarize, as a leader you need to set up and use your **ethical compass**, which refers to the set of values and goals that orient you toward appropriate decisions and behaviors.

Among the ethical values that you need to acknowledge as a leader in contemporary society, two are particularly important (and are also connected to each other): **sustainability** and **inclusion**.

The focus on sustainability

There are complex issues on a global scale—such as the deterioration of natural resources, climate change, regional crises and social tensions, poor access to education and healthcare, or technological disruptions—which require that leaders of companies, organizations, and institutions consider what is called the triple bottom line in defining and pursuing their goals.

The **triple bottom line** is a principle that encourages organizations (and especially businesses) to focus on their social and environmental performance—and not solely on financial results. It has three pillars—people, planet, and profit—that need to be preserved simultaneously:

- **Social sustainability**: create and distribute value for the good of society, 'giving back' to society in exchange for the resources that society provides to the organization, reciprocating in a fair way the provision of human capital and community resources.
- **Environmental sustainability**: preserve and restore the ecological system with the adoption of environmentally responsible practices.
- **Economic sustainability**: pursue the profits that are necessary for the organization to survive.

As a leader, to sharpen your focus on the triple bottom line you need to engage in a distinctive set of behaviors, such as: promoting a sustainable vision for your company; defining measurable outcomes for social responsibility; engaging and empowering diverse stakeholders; and setting clear ethical standards.[15]

You will also need to develop three key leadership competences that resemble the skills and competences that you encountered in Chapters

1 and 2, where we addressed the necessity for leaders to be able to solve wicked problems:[16]

- **A systems-thinking attitude.** Develop your ability to see reality as a complex network of things, events, and contexts, so you can evaluate decisions and consequences in a holistic, 'big picture' way.[17]
- **Relationship-building capabilities.** Build long-term relationships with key social, economic, and environmental stakeholders and promote cross-cultural dialogue; be sure to value the diversity of perspectives.
- **A sustainability mindset.** Nurture a strong sense of purpose and commitment in your team to meet the triple bottom line.

The focus on inclusion

Inclusion, in organizations and in society, consists of **providing fair access to opportunities and resources for people who might otherwise be excluded or marginalized**. This has become a fundamental ethical pillar, especially during the past decade, in connection with multiculturalism, diversity, and social sustainability.

Research has demonstrated that it is not what you can find in company mission statements and policies that makes a real difference in creating feelings of inclusion among people, but leadership. **Inclusive leaders** were found to share the following features:[18]

- **Visible commitment.** They are authentically committed to promoting diversity. This is reflected in behaviors like challenging the status quo, making others accountable for reaching inclusion-related goals and milestones, and making diversity and inclusion goals a personal priority.
- **Humility.** They are modest about themselves and their capabilities, ready to admit failures, and always willing to provide others with opportunities to contribute.
- **Awareness of bias.** They know their personal biases (or 'blind spots'), and they can recognize biased systems and work to correct them.
- **Curiosity about others.** They have an open attitude and show genuine curiosity about others.

- **Cultural intelligence.** They are aware of and adaptive to other cultures.
- **Effective collaboration.** They empower their followers, take different perspectives and ways of thinking into account, and promote a sense of safety to let everyone express their opinion, while at the same time staying focused on team cohesion.

Not surprisingly, these features resemble the leadership competences related to sustainability and developing a global mindset, and resonate with the key traits of transformational leadership too. Thus, the efforts that you need to make in developing the traits and skills that meet the different contemporary leadership challenges go mostly hand in hand and reinforce each other.

BEST PRACTICE

BUSINESS LEADERS WALKING THE TALK WHEN IT COMES TO INCLUSION[19]

Business leaders send a strong message when they demonstrate a commitment to diversity and inclusion that goes beyond rhetoric. A powerful example is Microsoft CEO Satya Nadella, who was named the 'top-rated CEO' for his diversity efforts based on a survey of non-white employees on the employee review site *Comparably* in 2020. The survey included questions about inclusion-related workplace factors (e.g. whether employees felt they were fairly paid).

Nadella has publicly addressed inclusion-related issues such as bias in artificial intelligence, the importance of racial and gender diversity, and female leadership in technology companies. He also linked the bonus system for top managers at Microsoft to diversity metrics, and puts a clear focus on the ability of senior managers to build a diverse team when discussing promotions.

In addition, Nadella set clear diversity and inclusion goals for Microsoft (e.g. to double the number of Black and African American leaders in the USA between 2020 and 2025), and has also made significant financial investments to achieve these goals (e.g. by adding an additional US$150 million to diversity and inclusion efforts from 2020 on).

"We need to ensure that our culture of inclusion is a top priority for everyone," wrote Nadella in an email to Microsoft employees, adding that "it starts with each of us making a commitment to do the work, to help drive change, and to act with intention."

Being equipped to navigate continuous change

Leadership is inherently about **change**. It is about envisioning a future state and making it happen.

Especially in today's turbulent environment, leaders need to be able to first create a readiness to change and then also realize change in organizational and social contexts, in order to both anticipate and respond to the frequent transformations and disruptions occurring in the economic, sociopolitical, and technological contexts.

The eight-step model for leading change

Researchers and management experts have proposed many models that suggest how you should promote and lead change.

One of the most established models is the **eight-step process for leading change**, introduced by management professor and change expert **John P. Kotter.**[20]

The model is inspired by earlier conceptualizations of the organizational change process, especially the view of change proposed by Kurt Lewin and adapted by Edgar Schein.[21]

Kotter suggests that in order to successfully lead change you need to follow these eight steps (see Figure 4.2 for a visualization of the model):[22]

1. **Create a sense of urgency.** Convince people that the change is needed for the organization's survival and growth. In this step, you need to understand the forces driving the need for change (e.g. are there internal pressures, such as new owners or an acquisition, or

external pressures, such as new competitors, new technologies, or new sociopolitical conditions?).

2. **Form a coalition.** Put together a team of people who endorse and support your effort toward change. In this team, you can include both internal and external stakeholders.

3. **Develop a vision and strategy.** Summarize the key ideas related to your change in a vision that people can easily understand, remember, and relate to. Once the motive and vision for change are understood, you need to create a plan that provides a roadmap of the change project, so that it is easier to communicate with your team, monitor the progress, and reorient if needed.

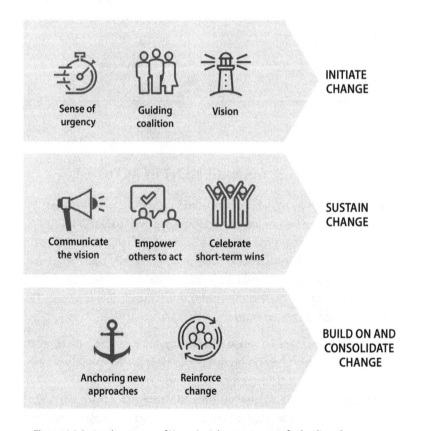

Figure 4.2 A visual summary of Kotter's eight-step process for leading change

4. **Communicate the vision.** Ensure that the vision is mentioned frequently, so that it becomes familiar to people. Call meetings to familiarize all the stakeholders involved with the plan.
5. **Deal with resistance.** Identify people and groups who are skeptical or resistant toward the change. Communicate and negotiate with them. Leverage people and groups who support the change to bring those who are doubtful on board.[23]
6. **Generate short-term wins.** Keep people motivated during the change process by highlighting short-term results.
7. **Build on the change.** Do not let people 'sit' on small, short-term wins, but keep striving toward the end goal.
8. **Stabilize the change.** Make sure that the change becomes part of your organization's culture and a natural part of the way people think and act.

BEST PRACTICE

CHANGE MANAGEMENT IN ACTION[24]

Alan Mulally served as CEO of the Ford Motor Company between 2006 and 2014. At the beginning of his tenure, he had to deal with massive losses and a declining market share. In what has later been called "the greatest corporate turnaround in US history," Mulally succeeded in getting Ford back on track and into a zone of stable profitability.

Mulally's actions during the Ford turnaround closely resemble key steps of Kotter's change model:

- Mulally first created a **sense of urgency**, for example with his statement "We have been going out of business for 40 years" in a meeting that was held with Ford employees early in his tenure.
- He then developed a **new vision and strategy** for the company. His 'One Ford' plan had four pillars: aggressively restructuring and chang-

ing the product mix to improve profitability, accelerating product development, securing a good financial base, and working together as one global team.

- In an effort to **form a coalition**, Mulally involved all important stakeholder groups, both internally and externally, as partners in the development and implementation of the 'One Ford' plan. That included customers and suppliers as well as investors, banks, and workers' unions.
- "His motto is communicate, communicate, communicate," wrote Gerhard Geyer, a former Ford executive, about Mullaly. He would use every chance to **communicate the vision**. He spoke very passionately about Ford's future in management meetings, and encouraged everyone to spread the message further. At the same time, he also tried to create a culture of transparency and openness, which facilitated the information flow throughout the corporation.
- The new open and transparent communication culture also created a sense of safety for the team, in the sense that it was ok to speak up and discuss problems. That helped to **deal with resistance**, because doubts, fears and problems could be openly voiced and discussed, and solutions could be found together. One manager, for example, reported a major problem with a new Ford model. Instead of reprimanding him, Mulally thanked the manager for this openness and asked others in the team to help him get the problem resolved.
- Mullaly knew about the importance of **generating short-term wins**, which included, for example, the quick arrangement of a 'survival loan' for the company, and the fast development and introduction of new successful models.
- Mulally did not rest on his early laurels, but continuously built on and **stabilized the change**. "Pretty relentless" is how Ford's chief financial officer described Mulaly, who rigorously followed up whether goals and targets were met, with weekly and sometimes even daily updates.

The agile approach to leading change

Kotter's eight-step model is especially appropriate for changes that you can plan carefully and lead with a top-down and sequential approach. However, in today's turbulent environment, there are changes that leave little time to plan. They might, for example, demand a fast response to a crisis, impose frequent modifications in the planned strategy, and require more 'bottom-up' initiatives.

These features are captured by the **agile view of change leadership**, which is reflected in the following principles:[25]

- **Foster the creation of self-organizing teams and 'local leaders.'** Especially when time is crucial and a response to a crisis is required, these teams can immediately address challenges and seize opportunities that are key to supporting the change (even if they are not yet visible to the top management).
- **Adopt and promote a 'test and learn' mindset and tools**, for example by setting up channels that enable you to continuously listen to stakeholders' sentiments (e.g. social media channels); by being prepared to allow modifications of the change initiative arising from the evaluation of new conditions as they emerge; or by using informal channels to update employees and stakeholders on the change process and on what is needed from them.
- **Establish a short-term accountability system.** If you plan frequent reporting and feedback sessions, you can provide real-time coaching and support, and can identify and communicate what is most needed from your team in that particular moment.
- **Be prepared to make quick decisions based on limited information**, by defining priorities, being action-oriented, and accepting mistakes (see the 'test and learn' point above).
- **Be personally responsible.** Especially if you are facing a crisis, you need to take personal ownership of the change that you ask of your team.

Leadership styles according to change type and stages

Another aspect that is not covered by the top-down and sequential models of change is the need for different leadership styles for different types and stages of change processes.

A useful model to refer to here is the classification of leadership styles provided by Goleman, Boyatzis, and McKee (mentioned in Chapter 1); we can consider which leadership styles are appropriate for different change processes:[26]

- **Coercive.** This style involves direction and command. Use it in a crisis—and even then only when absolutely needed. It is an appropriate style to employ if urgent changes are required instantly. Stress and mistrust may arise if this style is overused.
- **Authoritative.** This is the label that Goleman and his colleagues use to identify the 'visionary' style. It is useful in change processes that require long and sustained effort. It works best if you are genuinely enthusiastic about the change and have a positive relationship with your followers. It is also the style that we can ascribe to Alan Mulally (see the box on Mullaly above).
- **Affiliative.** This style is best if you need to restore relationships, overcome conflicts, and reestablish trust. It should always be used, however, in conjunction with other styles that set direction and create progress.
- **Democratic.** With this style you rely on your team's ability to self-direct and organize within a change, because you expect that they are able to come up with ideas to cope with the emerging features of the change. It can be seen as a mix of the participative and delegative (or laissez-faire) leadership styles discussed in Chapters 1 and 2.
- **Pacesetting.** This style combines leading by example and setting high standards. It is effective when you need to reach an ambitious target, and when you have a highly motivated and skilled team. Don't use it too much or for too long because it may create stress and exhaustion in the long term.
- **Coaching.** This is an appropriate style to use if individuals need to acquire new skills or knowledge as part of the changes being made.

As a change leader, you need to be aware that you may not have the abilities to use each and every style in an equally effective way. It is therefore important that you rely on **collaboration with trusted others** who can assist or supplement your leadership endeavor where necessary.

CONTEMPORARY LEADERSHIP CHALLENGES: A BRIEF SUMMARY IN 10 POINTS

1. The **most important contemporary challenges** you are likely to face as a leader are related to globalization and virtual connectivity, ethics, sustainability and inclusion, and turbulent change.

2. In a globalized world, you need to be aware that expectations regarding your role as a leader change according to the **cultural context** in which you operate. It is therefore important to cultivate your cultural mindset.

3. Global leadership across cultures is combined with the spatial and temporal dispersion of teams. Thus, knowing how to **lead virtual teams** has become a crucial challenge for leaders. Leading virtual teams requires specific adjustments to your leadership style.

4. As a leader, you can have a strong influence over other people and this implies a big **ethical responsibility.** You need to be prepared to act according to principles of honesty, justice, respect, community, and integrity, and also be able to solve ethical dilemmas.

5. Leadership ethics in the contemporary world are crucially linked to the values of **sustainability** and **inclusion.**

6. Sustainability implies that you consider the **triple bottom line** of social, environmental, and economic sustainability. This is facilitated if you develop a sustainability mindset, combined with relationship-building and systems-thinking capabilities.

7. As a leader, you need to be aware of the **importance of inclusion in organizations and society,** namely fair access to opportunities and resources for people who might otherwise be excluded or marginalized.

8. As a leader in today's turbulent environment, you need to be able to **create a readiness to change** and also be able to **realize change** in organizational and social contexts.

9. One of the most established models that can guide you in planning and executing change is the sequential **eight-step process for leading change**, introduced by John P. Kotter. In a crisis, you may need to adjust and adapt the sequential approach to change through the application of an **'agile' approach to leading change**.

10. Different types of change or **different stages of the change process require different leadership styles**. These are: coercive, authoritative/visionary, affiliative, democratic, pacesetting, and coaching.

••

Notes for Chapter 4

1   Hofstede, Hofstede, & Minkov (2005); Schein (2010).
2   Hofstede, Hofstede, & Minkov (2005).
3   Hall (1976); Trompenaars & Hampden-Turner (2012).
4   House, Hanges, Javidan, Dorfman, & Gupta (eds.) (2004).
5   Ibid.
6   Adapted from Javidan, Dorfman, De Luque, & House (2016).
7   Learn more about it from Nahavandi (2021).
8   Morrison-Smith & Ruiz (2020).
9   Lauring & Klitmøller (2016).
10 Kinsey Goman (2021); Malhotra, Majchrzak, & Rosen (2007).
11 Morgan (2008).
12 Bailenson (2021).
13 Yukl, Mahsud, Hassan, & Prussia (2013).
14 Chikeleze & Baehrend Jr. (2017).
15 D'Amato, Eckert, Ireland, Quinn, & Van Velsor (2010).
16 De Haan, Jansen, & Ligthart (2016).
17 Learn more about systems-thinking, sustainability, and wicked problems here: Meadows (2018).
18 Bourke, Titus, & Espedido (2020).
19 Based on information in Liu (2020); Nadella (2020).
20 Kotter (2012).
21 Schein (1996).
22 Kotter (2012).
23 There are also models that are specifically focused on overcoming resistance in leading change. An example is the ADKAR model (Awareness, Desire, Knowledge, Ability, Reinforcement). More about it can be found here: https://www.prosci.com/methodology/adkar.
24 Cable (2011); Geyer (2011); Miller Caldicott (2014); Taylor III (2009).
25 Clayton (2021).
26 Goleman, Boyatzis, & McKee (2013).

Leadership tools and techniques

» Recognize the prerequisites for effective leadership communication.
» Prepare and deliver an engaging leadership speech.
» Determine which decision-making style is the best fit in specific situations.
» Analyze and choose different approaches to managing and resolving conflicts.
» Use coaching techniques to help others develop and find solutions for their problems.
» Create your own leadership development plan.

There are a number of tools and techniques that can help you in developing, sharpening, and practicing your leadership skills to enhance your effectiveness in a leadership role. In this chapter, we will focus on the following:

- Leadership communication techniques
- Tools to identify and select the most appropriate decision-making approach
- Conflict management and negotiation techniques
- Coaching tools
- Tools for planning your personal leadership development

Communication techniques

Effective communication is essential for leadership. Research clearly indicates that through communication, leaders 'create reality' by giving particular meanings to problems and situations and effectively sharing these meanings with their followers.[1] This allows followers to align around a common vision and joint goals, and increase both their motivation and commitment.

Figure 5.1 Elements of effective leadership communication[4]

To communicate successfully as a leader, you need to consider the following aspects, which apply to both team and one-to-one communication (see also Figure 5.1):[2]

- **Adapt your communication style.** You need to be aware of your leadership style on the one hand and of the situation and audience on the other hand, and then adapt your communication style accordingly so these two aspects align. For example, if you have an authoritative style, you may be used to charismatic and one-way communication aimed at getting unconditional alignment from your followers. This may not be the best fit, however, if you address a group of people who are used to being more critical and having more autonomy and independence in their roles.

- **Decide what you're going to say in advance.** When you deliver important messages (whether to one person or many), make a clear plan for your communication, including ordering what you're going to say in a logical way.
- **Repeat.** To make sure they're absorbed and understood, deliver your messages multiple times. Research shows the importance of repeating communication to enhance effectiveness.[3]
- **Practice active listening.** Remember that communication is a two-way process. Listen carefully and focus on the other person, and do not think about what you are going to say while the other person is speaking. Instead of only listening 'with your ears,' you should also listen 'with your eyes' in order to capture non-verbal cues, too. Examples of active listening techniques include paraphrasing what the other person said (*"So, you want us to change supplier for the main components?"*) or asking open-ended questions (*"I understand you don't fully agree with the current decisions about the budgeting of the marketing campaign. What changes would you suggest instead?"*). Summarizing unclear discussions of difficult points is another good example of active listening.
- **Address everyone as individuals.** Work to deliver your message in such a way that the audience feels you are speaking to them individually. This could be done, for example, by identifying and 'studying' in advance the identity and the characteristics of the audience, so you can tailor your message more directly to them. Of course, this becomes easier when you communicate with your team. With your team members, you can also engage in non-business conversations in more informal settings, so they can relate to you, feel comfortable in sharing thoughts and ideas, and ultimately increase their trust.
- **Be authentic.** Be yourself and don't try to behave or look like someone else. Use a language that people can recognize as your own, and make your beliefs and values visible in your communication. Through authenticity you gain people's respect, because it conveys a message of honesty.

- **Pursue clarity.** Be clear rather than vague. Translate complex concepts into simple ideas your employees can relate to. Remember that if you find it difficult to break down a concept into its essential components, you may not have a clear understanding of it yourself. And if you don't understand something fully, you cannot communicate it in a credible and effective way.
- **Don't deliver monologues to your followers and to your team.** People are more willing to listen to you if they feel they have the opportunity to share their own ideas and opinions. Your aim should be to have dialogues with your followers.

A special type of communication: The 'leadership speech'

A leadership speech is a particular kind of communication that a leader uses to deliver, in a delimited amount of time, **a powerful message with the objective of inspiring followers and driving them toward a common goal.** The leadership speech is often needed to support and communicate a vision, which may be associated with goals of change and transformation at a personal, team, and organizational level (as we have seen in Chapters 3 and 4). For example, it could involve giving a 15-minute speech to the board to persuade them to support a strategic decision, or a 5-minute speech to your team to motivate them in the very last mile of a project.

BUILD YOUR LEADERSHIP SKILLS

HOW TO CREATE A VISION

According to the leadership scholar Gary Yukl, a vision is an idealistic picture of a desirable future that inspires a group or an organization, and "should appeal to the values, hopes, and ideals of organization members and other stakeholders whose support is needed."[5]

More specifically, the vision should:

- focus on reaching **long-term ideals and objectives** rather than short-term tangible results,
- foresee **an attainable future that is linked to the current reality** rather than being 'wishful thinking,'
- address **issues that are highly important for the organization and the stakeholders**, and
- be **as simple as possible** so it can be communicated concisely and clearly.

In practical terms, when you develop a vision statement (a compact summary of a vision in written form) you should keep in mind these simple guidelines:

- Preferably keep it shorter than two sentences and 30 words
- Be specific in your wording
- Use expressions that are relevant to your stakeholders
- Make it inspiring and ambitious
- Make it easy to remember

Here are some examples:

- Oxfam: *"We have a vision of a just and sustainable world."*
- LinkedIn: *"Create economic opportunity for every member of the global workforce."*
- The Coca-Cola Company: *"Loved brands, done sustainably, for a better shared future."*

As we can see from Oxfam and Coca-Cola's vision statements, more and more organizations are emphasizing their focus on sustainability (see also Chapter 4).

The function of the vision statement can also be fulfilled by purpose statements or mission statements, and a growing number of companies are relying on those types of statements to summarize their values and long-term goals.

To deliver an effective leadership speech, in addition to considering the general aspects of effective leadership communication outlined earlier in this chapter, you need to specifically focus on:

- The **structure and storyline** of the speech
- The use of **rhetorical devices**
- The use of your **voice and body language**

Let us now take a look at each of these elements of an effective leadership speech in a bit more detail.

The structure of a leadership speech

Giving a structure to your speech is a way to convey meaning and makes your message clearer and more memorable. There are several possible structures that you can use for organizing your communication, for example:

- **Situation—Complication—Resolution (SCR).**[7] You first present the current conditions in a transparent and unbiased way (situation). Then you interpret these current conditions in terms of a challenge (complication). The final part is the resolution, which illustrates or envisions a solution to the challenge.
- **Explanation.** The main purpose here is to inform about a plan, strategy, or process to address a problem or achieve something. You show the facts and combine them with storytelling or metaphors that clarify the facts.
- **Pitch.** Similar to the SCR structure, this is used to show how your idea can improve a situation. You illustrate a progression of events or facts leading to an obstacle that can ultimately be overcome thanks to an effective idea.
- **Drama.** This uses an inspirational story, such as how the company overcame various hardships in its early days, and then illustrates a positive outcome in terms of present or future success.
- **Situation—Opportunity—Resolution.** This is again similar to the SCR model. It reframes a complication as an opportunity, giving a positive slant to the challenge and encouraging taking action to resolve it.

- **Hook, Meat, and Payoff.** This structure is concerned with the progression of the communication rather than the content. You open your speech with a 'Hook': a catchy or surprising message to grab the attention of your audience. Then you provide the 'Meat,' by telling a story and delivering information in an interesting way. Finally, with the 'Payoff,' you give a 'rewarding' conclusion that inspires the audience.

If you are interested in learning more about how to structure a speech, check out the weblinks and video resources that you can on this book's companion website at *www.econcise.com/ConciseLeadershipTextbook.*

EXERCISE

DELIVER AN INSPIRATIONAL LEADERSHIP SPEECH

Prepare and practice giving a four-minute leadership speech (imagine that you are making the speech to your team). Choose one of the following four scenarios:

1. The new product launch has been a major success. You are addressing your team with the goal of letting them know that you need their full support in order to meet the increased demand, meaning they will all have to work overtime again, after a longer period of overtime in connection to the launch. Prepare a four-minute speech in which you explain your thinking.
2. Your division has been badly hit by the economic crisis. You need to lay off 10 percent of the workforce. Prepare a four-minute speech, where you make the announcement regarding the layoffs and address and motivate those who will remain.
3. The company where you work as a manager has been acquired by a big player in the industry. Your team is concerned about the possible changes ahead and the uncertainty over the company's future.

Prepare a four-minute speech in which you frame the changes ahead and motivate your team.

4. You have just been appointed as a project manager, and you are meeting your team for the first time. Prepare a four-minute speech in which you introduce yourself and tell them how you would like to lead the team.

The use of rhetorical devices

Rhetorical devices are techniques using language that aim to create a particular effect on the audience; they are often used to try to persuade people of something. Examples are figurative language, metaphors, and particular sentence structures.

Through **metaphors** and **figurative language**, you can get your message across more effectively because you create an image in people's minds. They can also relate your message to something familiar or appealing.

Common metaphors that are used in leadership speeches are those related to sports and games (e.g. to emphasize team effort, competition, and goals), to a journey (to emphasize perseverance and transformation), to war (to emphasize cohesion, endurance, and fierce competition), to machines (to emphasize order, reliability, or effectiveness in delivery), and to living organisms (to emphasize coordination, resilience, growth, and transformation).[8]

Another powerful rhetorical tool that dates back to the ancient civilizations of Greece and Rome is structuring sentences through particular techniques that **create repetition and rhythm** in the speech.

Two examples are:

- 'Tricolon,' which is a series of three phrases that resemble each other in wording, length, structure, and/or rhythm. You can use it to highlight your point in a memorable way. A commonly cited example is taken from former US president Barack Obama's speech at the Memorial Service for Nelson Mandela: *"And when the night grows dark, when injustice weighs heavy on our hearts, when our best-laid plans seem beyond our reach, let us think of Madiba and the words that brought him comfort within the four walls of his cell."*[9]

- 'Antithesis,' which is a contrast of two opposing ideas in the same sentence, or in two consecutive sentences. The contrast allows you to give focus to one of the ideas, which is normally the second one. Here's one example from former US president Richard Nixon's inaugural speech in 1969: "*We find ourselves rich in goods, but ragged in spirit; reaching with magnificent precision for the moon, but falling into raucous discord on earth. We are caught in war, wanting peace. We are torn by division, wanting unity.*"[10]

There are many more rhetorical devices that can be used to spice up your speech, such as **anaphora** (repeating the same word or phrase at the beginning of two or more sentences), **epistrophe** (repeating the same word or phrase at the end of two or more sentences), and **alliteration** (using words with the same letter or similar sound in a row).

The delivery of the speech: body and voice

According to research, the **non-verbal components of a speech**, such as tone of voice and body language, play a crucial role in effectively delivering the message.[11]

In a leadership role, you might want to pay particular attention to the following aspects:

- **Be loud and clear enough.** Project your voice to the back of the room.
- **Vary your tone.** Don't speak in monotone; vary the pitch of your voice to keep your listeners engaged.
- **Keep an appropriate pace.** In general, avoid speaking too quickly or too slowly, as both can frustrate your audience and make it harder for them to focus on what you're saying. The average suggested rate of speech is around 175 words per minute.[12]
- **But vary the pace in some parts of your speech.** For example, increase the pace to show enthusiasm, or slow down to convey emphasis or caution. Use pauses to let words resonate and give your audience a chance to reflect.
- **Maintain a good posture.** There is no universal rule here, but try to strike a balance between 'being yourself' and having a more 'formal'

posture. Do not exaggerate with 'power posing,'[13] but at the same time don't be too closed in with your body language. Open hand gestures signal receptivity.

- **Maintain eye contact.** Looking your audience directly in the eye (but not staring too much at a single person) helps build a sense of trust and personalizes your message.

Examples of powerful leadership speeches include New Zealand's prime minister Jacinda Arden's statement to the nation on COVID-19 in 2020, actress and activist Emma Watson's speech on gender equality at the United Nations in 2014, and former Apple founder and CEO Steve Jobs' Stanford commencement address in 2005. You can find weblinks to videos of these and other inspiring leadership speeches on the companion website of this book at *www.econcise.com/ConciseLeadershipTextbook*.

How to make decisions

As we have seen in Chapter 2, as a leader you are expected to make many decisions to solve all the problems that come your way. Although the 'content' of the decision-making process is different for every single problem, **the way you 'organize' the decision-making process** can be similar and can influence how effective it is.

In the following section, we will discuss two tools that are relevant here: the classification of **decision-making styles** and the **Vroom–Yetton–Jago model** of decision-making strategies.

Identify your decision-making style

Identifying your main decision-making style helps you to spot strengths, weaknesses, and potential areas for improvement. You can also use it to evaluate to what extent you can (or should) switch between styles.

Research has identified four styles that are relevant for leaders' decision making. These are:[14]

- **Analytical.** If you have this decision-making style, you are comfortable dealing with a large amount of information, even if it is ambiguous and contradictory. You want to find a comprehensive solution, so you may take a long time to make decisions. Your decisions are likely to be quite 'accurate,' but sometimes too 'costly' in terms of time.

- **Directive.** You prefer structure and you are results-oriented. You tend to make decisions quickly and prefer taking action rather than weighing different possibilities. You tend to rely on previous examples, experiences, and best practices to make decisions quickly. The comprehensiveness of the solution may be sacrificed, as well as other people's interests.

- **Conceptual.** You are comfortable with open-ended problems and options. You tend to see the 'big picture,' including interconnections (this style resembles the 'systems-thinking' attitude we encountered when we discussed sustainable leadership in Chapter 4). You lean toward creative ideas and holistic solutions. Sometimes, however, these solutions cannot be implemented quickly.

- **Behavioral.** You want to maintain interpersonal harmony during the process of decision making. You place a lot of emphasis on the opinions and needs of other people, seeking advice before proceeding toward a final decision. This makes others feel included and important. However, you may find it difficult to displease others. This can potentially bias your decision making and lead to sub-optimal outcomes that are ineffective for everyone (including you).

Remember that you can have more than one decision-making style. You may have a preferred style, but then also rely on other styles in specific situations (for example under stressful circumstances). It is also possible that you utilize a mix of styles, or that your style changes over time. As you continue to develop in your leadership role, you will have to learn to get comfortable with different styles.

WHAT IS YOUR DECISION-MAKING STYLE?

Indicate how far you agree with the following statements on a scale of 1–5, where 1 = *"I do not agree at all"*, 2 = *"I mainly disagree"*, 3 = *"I neither agree nor disagree"*, 4 = *"I mainly agree"*, and 5 = *"I fully agree"*.

	Statement	Your level of agreement (1-5)
1	I am comfortable with ambiguity.	
2	I am not scared by complex problems.	
3	The best decisions take time.	
4	I am not comfortable making decisions that may have a negative impact on the climate of my team.	
5	I prefer to take action.	
6	Relationships are the most valuable asset in the workplace.	
7	When making decisions, I think about the big picture.	
8	I am sensitive to new problems that emerge during the decision-making process.	
9	Before deciding, I often ask others "What do you think?"	
10	I can easily become frustrated when decisions require a lot of discussion between different people.	
11	Others often tell me that I am creative and have bold ideas.	
12	I don't necessarily need a black-or-white answer.	
13	I like to consider open-ended questions.	
14	I feel more efficient making decisions alone.	
15	Having to make decisions quickly makes me feel uncomfortable.	
16	I use rules, past results, and examples to make decisions.	
17	Others often tell me that I am a rational person.	
18	Before deciding I often ask others "How do you feel?"	
19	If I can gather more information, I'll make a better decision.	
20	I will change my decision if I foresee that people will react against it strongly and it will likely cause conflict.	

Now use the following table to count up the points that you gave for each group of statements. The totals (with a maximum of 25 points in each category) will indicate your preferred decision-making styles.

Question	Your points	Question	Your points	Question	Your points	Question	Your points
5		3		4		1	
10		8		6		2	
14		12		9		7	
16		15		18		11	
17		19		20		13	
Total DIRECTIVE		Total ANALYTICAL		Total BEHAVIORAL		Total CONCEPTUAL	

The Vroom-Yetton-Jago decision model

A tool that can complement your understanding of your personal decision-making styles is the model created by business psychologist and professor Victor H. Vroom and leadership professor Philip W. Yetton. It was later refined in collaboration with management professor Arthur G. Jago.[15]

Put simply, the model provides you with a checklist to assess when it is better to make a decision on your own, to inform your team, to gather input from your team, or to take a decision based on consensus.

First, you have to classify a decision according to the following factors:

- **Decision quality**: how important is to take the 'right' decision?
- **Information requirements**: do you have all the information needed or do you need to gather additional information from the team?
- **Team commitment and harmony**: what will be the impact of the decision on the team and does the team share the goals of the organization?
- **Team trust**: how likely is that the team will support a decision made on your own?
- **Problem structure**: is the problem well structured?

The way these factors combine make it more or less appropriate to use one of the following decision-making processes:

- **Autocratic 1 (A1)**: You don't require any input from your team. You use the information that you already have (e.g. from experience or benchmarks).
- **Autocratic 2 (A2)**: You consult with your team to get specific information that you don't have, then you make the final decision by yourself.
- **Consultative 1 (C1)**: You inform your team of the problem and interact individually with the members to ask for opinions. You make the final decision by yourself.
- **Consultative 2 (C2)**: You have a group discussion about the problem and get suggestions from the team. You then make the final decision by yourself.
- **Collaborative (G)**: You discuss the problem with your team and work actively to achieve a group consensus. You facilitate and steer the group toward a solution that they all agree on.

Table 5.1 shows the type of decision making that is more appropriate when different decision factors are present according to the model.

For each style, the table suggests the combination of factors that make that style more appropriate compared to the others. Cells with 'Y' (for 'Yes') indicate that the factor is present. Cells with 'N' (for 'No') indicate that the factor is absent. Blank cells indicate that the factor is not relevant for the selection of that style. For example, the first column tells you that: the importance of decision quality ('Y'), the unimportance of team commitment ('N'), and the availability of enough information to decide on your own ('Y') are sufficient factors to suggest the adoption of a A1 style, regardless of all the other conditions (blank).

Of course you don't have to blindly follow the prescriptions of the model. If you use it as a guideline, it can help you reflect on the most appropriate decision-making style without forgetting the specific features that characterize the context in which you operate.

	A1			A2					C1			C2				G				
The quality of the decision is important	Y	N	N	Y	Y	Y	Y	Y	Y	Y	Y	Y	Y	Y	Y	Y	N	Y	Y	Y
Team commitment to the decision is important	N	N	Y	Y	Y	Y	N	N	Y	N	Y	Y	Y	Y	N	Y	Y	Y	Y	Y
I have enough information to decide on my own	Y			Y	N	N	N	N	N	N		N	N	N	N	Y	N	N		
The problem is well structured				Y	Y	Y	Y	Y	Y	N	Y	N	N	N					N	Y
The team will support my individual decision				Y	Y	Y				Y		N	N	N	Y	N	N	N	N	
The team shares organizational goals				N	Y	N	Y	Y	Y	Y		N				Y	Y	Y		
There will be team conflict over the decision					N				N	Y	Y									Y

Table 5.1 Decision factors and the decision-making process according to the Vroom–Yetton–Jago model[16]

Conflict management and negotiation

Conflict management techniques help leaders to preserve interpersonal relationships, promote team cohesion, and encourage growth and learning at an individual and group level.

As a leader, you will face two types of conflict, which are often intertwined:[17]

1. **Task-related conflicts.** These relate to the team's goals and the methods used to meet those goals.
2. **Person-related (or relationship) conflicts.** These occur between individual team members and focus on personal aspects that are not necessarily connected to goals and tasks.

Person-related conflicts are usually more critical and difficult to resolve. They also tend to have a bigger negative impact on followers' job satisfaction, team morale, and performance.[18]

As a leader, you are expected to deal with serious conflicts emerging in your team. Here's how you can approach this (often quite challenging) task:

- **Recognize the potential causes of conflicts and try to prevent these from developing into actual conflicts.** There are many possible causes of conflict in an organizational setting (e.g. cultural and interpersonal differences; perceptions of unfair treatment, injustice, or an absence of equity; workload; poor communication and coordination; competition for scarce resources; adjustments to changing jobs and tasks; and so on). By identifying and understanding situations that could potentially lead to conflict, you can prepare in advance and develop plans to mitigate the impact of such circumstances. For example, you can help team members to better understand a process that if not understood correctly might create tension between them.
- **Develop codes of conduct and guidelines.** If you recognize behaviors that might later lead to conflicts (e.g. a confrontational attitude from a new team member), promote norms and rules that encourage a more respectful and collaborative environment.
- **Intervene only when it is necessary.** If the conflict has to do with a minor issue and/or the team members can solve it themselves, there is no need to invest time and energy in settling it, unless it persists for too long (which may pose a threat to the team climate).
- **Remain neutral and work collaboratively.** Clearly communicate to the parties involved in the conflict that you are not going to take a side but instead you will work together with them to find a solution that works for everybody.

It is important also to focus on **your own behavior in a conflict situation**. This applies, in particular (but not exclusively), in cases where you are one of the sides involved in the conflict (e.g. when one of your team members is directly arguing with you). Here's what you can do in such a situation:

- **Control your emotions and remain calm and professional.** For example, be aware of your own emotional triggers (see the exercise below) so that you can control them better, monitor the tone of your voice and body language, and direct your attention to the cause of conflict and shift it away from more personal aspects. When needed, you could also politely leave the meeting to let the situation de-escalate.

- **Establish boundaries when dealing with conflicts.** Recognize and communicate that the conflict is limited to a specific issue in a specific context, and should not spill over to affect the overall relationship among team members (or between you and the team member involved).
- **Understand and define the goals.** Identifying what each party wants helps you work toward a resolution. Open reflection on goals can foster the elaboration of a mutually beneficial or at least acceptable solution to the conflict.

EXERCISE

IDENTIFY YOUR EMOTIONAL TRIGGERS[19]

Emotional triggers are specific things that cause intense (usually negative) emotional responses. Triggers are more likely to emerge in emotionally intense situations, like open interpersonal conflict. They are connected to our previous experiences and memories that we 'reactivate' when we receive similar inputs.

Examples of attitudes or behaviors that can act as emotional triggers include, among others:

- Aggression
- Whining
- Crying
- Blaming others
- Ignoring others
- Lying
- Arrogance
- Anxiety
- Sadness

If your reaction to experiencing these attitudes or behaviors from someone else is particularly intense and negative, then the attitude or behavior is an emotional trigger.

Using the list above as inspiration, identify your own emotional trigger(s). Think about the memories and experiences from your personal life that you attach to each trigger, and consider your usual reaction to the trigger. What form does the reaction take? Why does it emerge?

This exercise can help you to keep your reactions to emotional triggers under control when they arise the next time.

Conflict resolution as a negotiation

Conflict occurs when the interests and goals of people are not aligned. Resolving a conflict requires conflicting parties finding an **agreement** that reconciles the divergent interests.

This agreement is typically the outcome of a **negotiation process**. We can therefore consider negotiation to be a conflict resolution strategy.

There are different approaches that you can adopt as a leader to reach or promote an agreement, both in the context of a conflict and in a more general negotiation setting. These **general conflict resolution (and negotiation) strategies** are:[20]

- **Competing.** If you choose this strategy, you expect a 'win-lose' result, meaning that one party will gain more than the other from the resolution. This strategy requires you to be assertive and committed to getting results. It involves an aggressive approach and the use of 'hard bargaining' negotiation tactics.[21] It may be not helpful if you expect to have a long-term relationship with the other party.
- **Avoiding.** This strategy implies neutrality, objectivity, and detachment from the situation. It also means that the responsibility for the negotiating process is given to the other party. If you use this strategy it might mean that you are open to a 'self-sacrifice', thus avoiding could easily lead to a 'lose-win' result (where the other party wins), but also to a 'lose-lose' result if your avoidance sabotages the negotiation.

- **Accommodating.** If you choose this strategy, your main focus is on maintaining a good relationship with the other party. You will work to minimize differences and reduce friction. The substance of the agreement will have a lower priority than the quality of the relationship.
- **Compromising.** This is your strategy if you aim for a middle-ground outcome, and you pursue this goal by asking for and obtaining concessions and accepting mutual losses that signal goodwill from both parties. This strategy is focused on creating an acceptable agreement while maintaining a stable relationship.
- **Collaborating.** With this approach, your goal is to 'work as a team' with the other party to find creative solutions that resolve the conflict. You may need to expand the scope of the negotiation to fully satisfy the interests of all parties. You put emphasis on the generation of many ideas and on the creation of long-term value.

More resources (weblinks and video links) on negotiations and conflict resolution can be found on the companion website of this book at *www.econcise.com/ConciseLeadershipTextbook.*

Coaching as a leadership tool

The contemporary challenges outlined in Chapter 4 suggest that leaders increasingly need to empower followers by offering them support and guidance in the development of competences and problem-solving skills, as well as in assuming a proactive solution-oriented attitude.

This means that in your leadership role, you need to familiarize yourself with **coaching techniques**.

Coaching is a purposeful interaction in which one person (the *coach* or in our context the coaching leader) uses a questioning approach to help another person (the *coachee* or follower who is being coached) to take the appropriate actions to realize their full potential and achieve their personal or professional goals.[22]

The coaching conversation is at the core of your coaching task as a leader. It's a **dialogue** aimed at supporting the coachee in their thinking and learning process.

The GROW model

A widely used method for designing coaching conversations is the GROW model, developed by former professional racing driver and business and leadership consultant Sir John Whitmore.[23]

Figure 5.2 The GROW model[25]

GROW (see Figure 5.2) is an acronym that stands for:

- **Goal**: "What does the coachee want to achieve?"
- **Reality**: "What does the current situation look like?"
- **Options**: "What are the alternative courses of action for improving the situation?"
- **Will**: "What will the coachee actually do to improve the situation? Which concrete action steps will they take?"

Let's look at each component in further detail.[26]

Goal

As a coaching leader, you need to develop a clear common understanding of what the follower would actually like to accomplish.

In a coaching process there are two types of goals:

- **Inspirational end goals**: what the coachee would like to achieve in the long term (for example, a runner wants to run the New York Marathon in three years from now).
- **Specific performance goals**: clearly defined smaller goals that bring the coachee closer to reaching their end goal (for example, within the next three months the aspiring marathon runner needs to increase the distance they run from five to ten kilometers).

Through coaching conversations you want to agree on the end goal that the coachee wants to reach, and to define intermediate performance goals (ideally not more than three) that the coachee needs to achieve in order to be able to reach the end goal.

Reality

This step of the conversation is aimed at objectively **assessing the situation together**. It means that the coach and coachee should rely on facts rather than just on personal feelings about a certain situation.

For example, the conversation can focus on factors influencing the current performance of the follower, with questions like *"In what way did your actions contribute to these results?"* or *"What obstacles have hindered your progress so far?"* This will increase the coachee's self-awareness of their own role in specific situations, and also of their potential to actually 'make a difference' in how things unfold.

The 'Reality' step also helps the coachee acknowledge that there is an **external reality** (e.g. other people, structures, power relationships, norms and rules) interacting with the coachee's **internal reality** (e.g. personal values, expectations, attitudes, or feelings). The encounter between these two realities may generate anxiety and fear in the coachee, for example because of the threat of negative consequences associated with certain actions or failures. These fears often remain hidden and unexpressed.

It is your role as a leader to discover and discuss with your follower those factors that create anxiety and fear through the tension between external and internal reality.

Options

In this phase, you and your coachee generate different **alternatives for reaching the coachee's goals**. Both you and your coachee can (and often need to be) creative in this phase.

At this point in time, you should both consider options regardless of how feasible they are (in terms of potentially being constrained by money, time, regulations, etc.). This allows you to identify more creative solutions.

As a coach, you can ask questions that stimulate more ideas from the coachee, and also contribute your own ideas, possibly fostering further inputs and thoughts from the coachee.

In general, the more options you have, the better. But at the same time, you should avoid information overload. A general guideline is that three to five serious options are a reasonable number to be considered and explored in an effective discussion. So, after an initial brainstorming session, only the most promising ideas should be considered further.

Among these ideas, you and your coachee would identify the strengths and weaknesses of each one.

Will

The final step of the GROW coaching process is deciding which option to pursue and developing an action plan. 'Will' refers to the intention of the coachee to take certain concrete actions (*"I will do ..."*).

Ideally, this phase will lead to a decision of **what the coachee will do**, a specific timeframe for the actions they will take, and an idea of how the coachee will overcome any obstacles along the way.

It is important to stress that in this stage as a coaching leader, you shouldn't push your follower in a certain direction, but rather **support them in finding their own way** and creating a workable plan.

The outcome of the 'Will' phase, other than the action plan itself, is a joint assessment of the coachee's commitment to the plan. One way to 'materialize' and thus increase the coachee's commitment toward the actions is to write down the planned actions on a 'next steps list,' and then have this list formally shared between the coach and the coachee, for example via email.

EXAMPLES OF COACHING QUESTIONS[27]

Questions for the 'Goal' phase:

- *"What exactly would you like to accomplish?"*
- *"What is your ultimate goal? What would things look like if you achieve it?"*
- *"What makes this goal so important for you?"*
- *"What are the main milestones on the way to achieving this goal?"*
- *"How could you set a goal so it primarily depends on your own actions and performance rather than on the circumstances or on what others do?"*
- *"How will you measure success?"*

Questions for the 'Reality' phase:

- *"What are the main factors that contributed to this situation?"*
- *"Who else is involved in this issue? What is their role?"*
- *"Which steps have you already taken to tackle this issue?"*
- *"What happened as a consequence?"*
- *"What are the main obstacles?"*
- *"What are your main concerns?"*
- *"What holds you back from taking action?"*

Questions for the 'Options' phase:

- *"What could be a potential solution here?"*
- *"What choices do you have?"*
- *"What advice would you give to someone else who is in the same situation as you are?"*
- *"What did you do when you were in a similar situation before?"*
- *"What could you do to remove this obstacle?"*
- *"How would you proceed if you had more money/time/information/...?"*
- *"Who could help you here?"*
- *"Which of these options do you see as the most promising one (and why)?"*

Prepare your personal leadership development plan

A **personal leadership development plan** is a very useful tool that you can adopt to define and keep track of goals and progress in your development as a leader.

Here's how you can create your own development plan:

- Start by **crafting a personal vision** on why you desire to grow as a leader and what kind of leadership profile you want to achieve (and how this would fit in with your future professional career).
- Then proceed with **identifying your current leadership traits, skills, competences, behaviors, and experiences** (see also Chapter 2) and assessing your strengths and weaknesses. In this stage, you could rely on other people's feedback: friends, trusted peers (colleagues or fellow students), or someone who is coaching or mentoring you.
- Once you have identified your specific strengths and weaknesses, identify up to a maximum of four **areas where you need to develop/ grow/improve** and **formulate key objectives** linked to these areas, which you can preferably achieve within one to three years. For example, you may want to: 1) clearly identify and consolidate your leadership style; 2) focus on improving your problem-solving skills; or 3) improve your communication skills.
- Define, in a detailed timeline, **specific goals for each objective** as well as **actions to take and resources or support needed**. Don't forget to consider potential obstacles that might derail your plan,

and ways to assess whether you're making enough (or the right type of) progress. In doing this, you will benefit from the adoption of a SMART approach (see the box below).

HOW TO BECOME A SMART GOAL-SETTER

SMART is an acronym of five criteria that can help you to set clear goals that are easier to achieve.

- Your goals (and plan) need to be **specific**, rather than based on vague or broad statements. The more specific your goals, the more likely you'll implement them effectively.
- Your plan needs to include **measurable** results. Results must be quantifiable or objectively observable through documented milestones or achievements. In other words, your plan should have key performance indicators (KPIs) related to your objectives.
- You need to set **achievable** goals. While aiming high is laudable, you should avoid setting targets that are too ambitious and impossible to achieve.
- The goals need to be **relevant** so they complement one another and synergize with other aims in your professional life.
- Finally, the implementation of the plan needs to be **time-bound**. You need to set a specific time frame for taking actions and measuring results.

Remember that your leadership development plan can be adjusted in order to remain relevant if external circumstances change or unforeseen events and opportunities occur. Also consider your first one-to-three year leadership development plan only as a first step, possibly followed by subsequent plans that build on the achievements of the previous ones.

You can create a plan at different stages of your career, pursuing different aims. For example:

- **Early career**: establish what it means to be a leader and identify potential opportunities
- **Mid-career**: reflect on previous leadership experiences and reconsider opportunities
- **Late career**: assess if and how your leadership profile and approach have changed
- **New organization or new role**: examine how your leadership profile fits with the new situation

You can find a template for creating your personal leadership development plan in Table 5.2 below.

Objective	Specific goals	Actions to reach the goal	Resources and support needed to reach the goal	Planned timeline to reach the goal	Potential obstacles in the pursuit of the goal	Key performance indicators	Responsibility for the evaluation
Improve problem-solving techniques as a leader	Acquire knowledge of analytical decision-making tools	Participate in formal training initiatives and courses	Support from the immediate manager at work	Within the next 12 months	Limited time to prepare course assignments	Certification of successful course completion	Self-evaluation; mentor
	Acquire creative thinking skills	...	...	...	...	...	...

Table 5.2 Example of a simple template for a leadership development plan

In your leadership development plan you can include goals at different levels, ranging from deepening your knowledge and understanding of leadership, to the practical application of that knowledge to specific contexts and problems, to the acquisition of specific technical skills that complement your personal portfolio.

LEADERSHIP TOOLS AND TECHNIQUES:
A BRIEF SUMMARY IN 10 POINTS

1. **Effective communication** is essential for leadership, because it allows followers to align around a common vision and joint goals, and increase both their motivation and commitment.

2. A particular kind of communication is the **leadership speech.** You can use it to deliver a powerful message with the objective of inspiring followers and driving them toward a common goal.

3. When preparing and delivering a leadership speech you need to focus on: the **structure and storyline of the speech**; the use of **rhetorical devices**; and the use of **voice and body language**.

4. The way you 'organize' the **decision-making process** is an important aspect of solving problems. The classification of decision-making styles and the Vroom–Yetton–Jago model of decision-making strategies are useful tools for structuring your approach to decision making.

5. Identifying your **main decision-making style** can help you to spot strengths, weaknesses, and potential areas for improvement. You can also use it to evaluate to what extent you can (or should) switch between styles. There are four relevant styles: analytical, directive, conceptual, and behavioral.

6. The **Vroom–Yetton–Jago model** provides you with guidelines for choosing a decision-making style, where each style involves the followers to a different degree in the decision making (autocratic, consultative, and collaborative styles).

7. **Conflict management techniques** help you to preserve high-quality relationships with your followers, and also encourage growth and learning at the individual and group level. It is important to prepare for potential conflicts and also to focus on your own behavior in a conflict.

8. Conflict resolution implies a successful **negotiation** between competing interests. Basic conflict resolution often relies on basic negotiation strategies, which are: competing, avoiding, accommodating, compromising, and collaborating.

9. As a leader, you need to empower followers by offering them support and guidance in the development of competences and problem-solving skills, as well as in assuming a proactive solution-oriented attitude. This requires you to familiarize yourself with **coaching techniques**. The **GROW model** is a key tool for framing your coaching conversations.

10. It is important that you define and keep track of goals and progress in your development as a leader. That's why it is helpful to develop a **personal leadership development plan**, inspired by the SMART goal-setting principles.

Notes for Chapter 5

1   Ruben & Gigliotti (2016).
2   Landry (2019).
3   Neeley & Leonardi (2011).
4   Inspired by contents in Landry (2019).
5   Yukl (2013), p. 89.
6   Yukl (2013).
7   This storyline is commonly associated with the management consultancy firm McKinsey & Company.
8   Mayer-Schoenberger & Oberlechner (2002).
9   Obama (2013).
10 Washington Post (January 21 1969, page A01).
11 Darioly & Mast (2013).
12 Baker & Warren (2015).
13 Cuddy, Wilmuth, & Carney (2012).
14 Rowe & Boulgarides (1992).
15 Vroom & Jago (1988); Vroom & Yetton (1973)
16 Inspired by contents in Vroom & Yetton (1973); Vroom & Jago (1988).
17 Pinkley (1990).
18 De Dreu & Weingart (2003).
19 Inspired by contents in https://www.workplacestrategiesformentalhealth.com/resources/emotional-triggers, accessed July 5 2022.
20 Thomas (1976).
21 See, for example, Harvard Law School Program on Negotiation Staff (2021).
22 Sternad (2021).
23 Whitmore (2010).
24 Sternad (2021).
25 Sternad (2021), p. 29 (inspired by concepts in Whitmore (2017)). Illustration source: pixabay.com.
26 Parts of the text in the rest of this section are based on Sternad (2021).
27 The questions are taken from Sternad (2021).

A concluding note

Through reading this book, you have learned about principles, ideas, methods, and techniques related to leadership. You have also become more reflective and self-aware about how to develop as a leader.

I really hope that a few key messages from this book will accompany you on your future leadership development path:

- **Good leadership practices are rooted in extensive knowledge and research** about individuals, groups, and organizations.
- **Everyone can be a leader who makes a difference.** Leadership is about working with other people to solve problems—and about doing good and changing things for the better for your team, your organization, and your community.
- **Effective leadership is connected to the ability to solve wicked problems** and address the increasingly complex challenges of our era.

If this concise textbook has contributed to your own learning and development, and if you think it could also benefit your colleagues, team members, fellow students, or friends, please do suggest it to them too.

I'd also be grateful if you could write **an honest online review.** Taking just a few minutes to write two or three sentences could really help this book to reach a wider audience, and enable the publisher to continue producing approachable and affordable textbooks like this one.

The more people who learn about the subject of leadership and its related challenges, the higher the chances are that great new leaders will emerge—leaders with the willingness and ability to work for a better future. Thank you for being one of them!

Bibliography

Bailenson, J. N. (2021). Nonverbal overload: A theoretical argument for the causes of Zoom fatigue. *Technology Mind and Behavior, 2*(1). https://doi.org/10.1037/tmb0000030.

Baker, T., & Warren, A. (2015). *Conversations at Work: Promoting a Culture of Conversation in the Changing Workplace*. London: Palgrave Macmillan.

Bass, B. M. & Avolio, B. J. (eds.). (1994). *Improving Organizational Effectiveness Through Transformational Leadership*. Thousand Oaks, CA: Sage Publications.

Blake, R. R., Mouton, J. S., & Bidwell, A. C. (1962). Managerial grid. *Advanced Management-Office Executive, 1*(9), 12–15.

Blake, R. R., & Mouton, J. S. (1978). What's new with the grid*? *Training and Development Journal, 32*(5), 3–8.

Bourke, J., Titus, A., & Espedido, A. (2020). The key to inclusive leadership. *Harvard Business Review*, https://hbr.org/2020/03/the-key-to-inclusive-leadership, published 6 March 2020, accessed 3 July 2022.

Bowers, D. G., & Seashore, S. E. (1966). Predicting organizational effectiveness with a four-factor theory of leadership. *Administrative Science Quarterly, 11*(2), 238–263.

Buffett, W. (1998). Lecture at the University of Florida School of Business. https://vintagevalueinvesting.com/wp-content/uploads/2017/01/Warren-Buffett-University-of-Florida-Lecture-Vintage-Value-Investing.pdf, accessed 16 May 2022.

Burns, J. M. (1978). *Leadership*. New York: Harper & Row.

Cable, J. (2011). Management lessons you can learn from Alan Mullaly. https://www.industryweek.com/the-economy/article/21953589/management-lessons-you-can-learn-from-alan-mulally, published 30 June 2011, accessed 5 July 2022.

Cain, S. (2012). *Quiet: The Power of Introverts in a World that Can't Stop Talking*. New York, NY: Crown Publishers.

Cain, S., Mone, G., & Moroz, E. (2016). *Quiet Power: The Secret Strengths of Introverts*. New York, NY: Penguin.

Chikeleze, M. C., & Baehrend Jr, W. R. (2017). Ethical leadership style and its impact on decision-making. *Journal of Leadership Studies, 11*(2), 45–47.

Clayton, S. J. (2021). An agile approach to change management. *Harvard Business Review*. https://hbr.org/2021/01/an-agile-approach-to-change-management, published 12 January 2021, accessed 5 July 2022.

Costa, P. T., & McCrae, R. R. (1999). A five-factor theory of personality. In Pervin, L. A., & Oliver, J. P. (eds). *Handbook of Personality: Theory and Research*, 2nd ed. (pp. 139–153). New York, NY: Guilford Press.

Cuddy, A. J., Wilmuth, C. A., & Carney, D. R. (2012). The benefit of power posing before a high-stakes social evaluation. *Harvard Business School Working Paper Series* #13-027.

Cunningham, L. A. (2014). *The Essays of Warren Buffett: Lessons for Investors and Managers*, 4th ed. Hoboken, NJ: Wiley.

D'Amato, A., Eckert, R., Ireland, J., Quinn, L., & Van Velsor, E. (2010). Leadership practices for corporate global responsibility. *Journal of Global Responsibility, 1*(2), 225–249.

Darioly, A., & Mast, M. S. (2013). The role of nonverbal behavior in leadership: An integrative review. In: Riggion, R. E., & Tan, S. J. (eds), *Leader Interpersonal and Influence Skills* (pp. 73–100). London: Routledge.

De Cremer, D., & Tao, T. (2015). Leadership innovation: Huawei's rotating CEO system, https://www.europeanbusinessreview.com/leadership-innovation-huaweis-rotating-ceo-system/, published 20 November 2015, accessed 30 June 2022.

De Dreu, C. K., & Weingart, L. R. (2003). Task versus relationship conflict, team performance, and team member satisfaction: A meta-analysis. *Journal of Applied Psychology, 88*(4), 741-49.

De Haan T., Jansen P., & Ligthart P. (2016). Sustainable leadership: Talent requirements for sustainable enterprises. https://www.russellreynolds.com/en/insights/reports-surveys/sustainable-leadership-talent-requirements-for-sustainable-enterprises, published 21 January 2016, accessed 2 July 2022.

Denis, J. L., Langley, A., & Sergi, V. (2012). Leadership in the plural. *Academy of Management Annals, 6*(1), 211–283.

DeRue, D. S., & Ashford, S. J. (2010). Who will lead and who will follow? A social process of leadership identity construction in organizations. *Academy of Management Review, 35*(4), 627–647.

Development Dimensions International, Inc. (2016). High-resolution leadership: A synthesis of 15,000 assessments into how leaders shape the business landscape. https://media.ddiworld.com/research/high-resolution-leadership-2015-2016_tr_ddi.pdf, accessed 14 May 2022.

Drucker, P. F. (1974). *Management: Tasks, Responsibilities, Practices.* New York, NY: Harper & Row.

Drucker, P. F. (1996). *The Executive in Action: Managing for Results, Innovation and Entrepreneurship.* New York, NY: HarperCollins.

Dyer, J., Furr, N., & Lefrandt, C. (2019). *Innovation Capital: How to Compete—and Win—Like the World's Most Innovative Leaders.* Boston, MA: Harvard Business Review Press.

Elkins, K. (2017). 11 of Warren Buffett's funniest and most frugal quirks. https://finance.yahoo.com/news/11-warren-buffett-apos-funniest-155736508.html, published 9 May 2017, accessed 16 May 2022.

Eurich, T. (2018). What self-awareness really is (and how to cultivate it). *Harvard Business Review*, https://hbr.org/2018/01/what-self-awareness-really-is-and-how-to-cultivate-it, published 4 January 2018, accessed 14 May 2022.

Fayol, H. (1949). *General and Industrial Management.* Oxford: Oxford University Press.

Fiedler, F. E. (1964). A contingency model of leadership effectiveness. In: Berkowitz, L. (ed.), *Advances in Experimental Social Psychology*, Vol. 1 (pp. 149–190). New York, NY: Academic Press.

French, J. P. R. Jr. & Raven, B. (1968). The bases of social power. In: Cartwright, D. & Zander, A. F. (eds), *Group Dynamics: Research and Theory*, 3rd ed. (pp. 259–269). New York, NY: Harper & Row.

Geyer, G. (2011). *Ford Motor Company: The Greatest Corporate Turnaround in U.S. History.* Seattle, WA: CreateSpace.

Goleman, D., Boyatzis, R. E., & McKee, A. (2013). *Primal Leadership: Unleashing the Power of Emotional Intelligence*. Boston, MA: Harvard Business Review Press.

Graen, G. B., & Uhl-Bien, M. (1995). Relationship-based approach to leadership: Development of leader–member exchange (LMX) theory of leadership over 25 years: Applying a multi-level multi-domain perspective. *The Leadership Quarterly, 6*(2), 219–247.

Grant, A. M., Gino, F., & Hofmann, D. A. (2011). Reversing the extraverted leadership advantage: The role of employee proactivity. *Academy of Management Journal, 54*(3), 528–550.

Greenleaf, R. K. (1998). *The Power of Servant-Leadership: Essays*. Oakland, CA: Berrett-Koehler Publishers.

Grint, K. (2010). *Leadership: A Very Short Introduction*. Oxford: Oxford University Press.

Hackman, J. R. (2010). What is this thing called leadership? In: Nohria, N., & Khurana, R. (eds), *Handbook of Leadership Theory and Practice*. Boston, MA: Harvard Business Press.

Hall, E. (1976). *Beyond Culture*. New York, NY: Anchor Press.

Harvard Law School Program on Negotiation Staff (2021). 10 hard-bargaining tactics to watch out for in a negotiation. https://www.pon.harvard.edu/daily/batna/10-hardball-tactics-in-negotiation/, published 11 October 2021, accessed 5 July 2022.

Hermann, A., & Gulzar Rammal, H. (2010). The grounding of the "flying bank." *Management Decision, 48*(7), 1048–1062

Hersey, P., & Blanchard, K. H. (1969). Life cycle theory of leadership. *Training & Development Journal, 23*(5), 26–34.

Hickman, G. R., & Sorenson, G. J. (2013). *The Power of Invisible Leadership: How a Compelling Common Purpose Inspires Exceptional Leadership*. Thousand Oaks, CA: Sage Publications.

Hofstede, G., Hofstede, G. J., & Minkov, M. (2005). *Cultures and Organizations: Software of the Mind*, 2nd ed. New York, NY: McGraw Hill.

House, R. J. (1996). Path–goal theory of leadership: Lessons, legacy, and a reformulated theory. *The Leadership Quarterly, 7*(3), 323–352.

House, R. J., Hanges, P. J., Javidan, M., Dorfman, P. W., & Gupta, V. (eds) (2004). *Culture, Leadership and Organizations: The GLOBE Study of 62 Societies*. Thousand Oaks, CA: Sage.

Huawei.com (2022). Corporate governance overview. https://www.huawei.com/en/corporate-governance, accessed 30 June 2022.

Janis, I. (1982). *Groupthink*, 2nd ed. Boston, MA: Houghton-Mifflin.

Javalagi, A., & Newman, D. A. (2021). Cross-cultural collectivism supports extraversion and agreeableness leadership advantage, *Academy of Management Proceedings*, Vol. 2021, No. 1, DOI: https://doi.org/10.5465/AMBPP.2021.16418abstract.

Javidan, M., Dorfman, P. W., De Luque, M. S., & House, R. J. (2016). In the eye of the beholder: Cross-cultural lessons in leadership from Project GLOBE. In: Reiche, B. S., Stahl, G. K., Mendenhall, M. E., & Oddou, G. R. (eds), *Readings and Cases in International Human Resource Management* (pp. 119–154). London: Routledge.

Judge, T. A., Bono, J. E., Ilies, R., & Gerhardt, M. W. (2002). Personality and leadership: A qualitative and quantitative review. *Journal of Applied Psychology, 87*(4), 765–780.

Judge, T. A., Erez, A., Bono, J. E., & Thoresen, C. J. (2003). The core self-evaluations scale: Development of a measure. *Personnel Psychology, 56*(2), 303–331.

Kaiser, R. B., LeBreton, J. M., & Hogan, J. (2015). The dark side of personality and extreme leader behavior. *Applied Psychology: An International Review, 64*(1), 55–92.

Karelaia, N., & Van der Heyden, L. (2020). Leadership in wicked times. INSEAD Knowledge. https://knowledge.insead.edu/leadership-organisations/leadership-in-wicked-times-15286, published 13 October 2020, accessed 13 April 2022.

Katz, R. L. (1974). Skills of an effective administrator. *Harvard Business Review*, 52(5), 90–102.

Kinsey Goman, C. (2021). How to keep your virtual team from tuning out. https://www.forbes.com/sites/carolkinseygoman/2021/10/15/how-to-keep-your-virtual-team-from-tuning-out/, published 15 October 2021, accessed 1 July 2022.

Klopp, J. (2010). "Wer das Fressen gibt, ist der Chef" (interview). *Impulse magazine*, 6/2010, 22-23.

Kotter, J. P. (2012). *Leading Change*. Boston, MA: Harvard Business Press.

Kouzes, J. M., & Posner, B. Z. (2007). *The Leadership Challenge*, 4th ed. San Francisco: Jossey-Bass.

Landry L. (2019). 8 essential leadership communication skills. *Harvard Business School Online Business Insights*. https://online.hbs.edu/blog/post/leadership-communication, published 14 November 2019, accessed 5 July 2022.

Lauring J., & Klitmøller A. (2016) Global leadership competences for the future: Virtual collaboration. Research Report. Aahrus: Aarhus University/University of Southern Denmark/Global Leadership Academy.

Lewin, K., Lippit, R. & White, R. K. (1939). Patterns of aggressive behavior in experimentally created social climates. *Journal of Social Psychology, 10*(2), 269–299.

Liu, J. (2020). These are the best CEOs for diversity, according to employee reviews. https://www.cnbc.com/2020/07/20/the-best-ceos-for-diversity-according-to-comparably-employee-reviews.html, published 20 July 2020, accessed 4 July 2022.

Luscombe, B. (n.d.). Life after death. https://time.com/sheryl-sandberg-option-b/, accessed 25 July 2022.

Malhotra, A., Majchrzak, A., & Rosen, B. (2007). Leading virtual teams. *Academy of Management Perspectives, 21*(1), 60–70.

Mayer-Schoenberger, V., & Oberlechner, T. (2002). Through their own words: Towards a new understanding of leadership through metaphors. *SSRN working paper*. DOI 10.2139/ssrn.357542

Meadows, D. (2018). *Thinking in Systems*, 2nd ed. Hartford, VT: Chelsea Green Publishing Co.

Miller Caldicott, S. (2014). Why Ford's Alan Mulally is an innovation CEO for the record books. https://www.forbes.com/sites/sarahcaldicott/2014/06/25/why-fords-alan-mulally-is-an-innovation-ceo-for-the-record-books/?sh=5ae9fde47c04, published 25 June 2014, accessed 5 July 2022.

Morgan, N. (2008). *Trust Me: Four Steps to Authenticity and Charisma*. San Francisco, CA: Jossey Bass.

Morrison-Smith, S., & Ruiz, J. (2020). Challenges and barriers in virtual teams: A literature review. *SN Applied Sciences, 2*(6), 1–33.

Mullins, J., & Komisar, R. (2009). *Getting to Plan B: Breaking Through to a Better Business Model.* Boston, MA: Harvard Business Press.

Mumford, M. D., & Connelly, M. S. (1991). Leaders as creators: Leader performance and problem solving in ill-defined domains. *The Leadership Quarterly, 2*(4), 289–315.

Mumford, M. D., Zaccaro, S. J., Harding, F. D., Jacobs, T. O., & Fleishman, E. A. (2000). Leadership skills for a changing world: Solving complex social problems. *The Leadership Quarterly, 11*(1), 11–35.

Nadella, S. (2020). Addressing racial injustice. *Microsoft Corporate Blogs.* https://blogs.microsoft.com/blog/2020/06/23/addressing-racial-injustice/, published 23 June 2020, accessed 4 July 2022.

Nahavandi, A. (2009). *The Art and Science of Leadership*, 5th ed. Upper Saddle River, NJ: Pearson Prentice Hall.

Nahavandi, A. (2021). *The Cultural Mindset: Managing People Across Cultures.* Thousand Oaks, CA: SAGE Publications.

Neeley, T., & Leonardi, P. (2011). Effective managers say the same thing twice (or more). *Harvard Business Review, 89*(5), 38–39.

Northouse, P. G. (2021). *Leadership: Theory and Practice*, 9th ed. Thousand Oaks, CA: Sage Publications.

Obama, B. (2013). Remarks by President Obama at Memorial Service for former South African President Nelson Mandela. https://obamawhitehouse.archives.gov/the-press-office/2013/12/10/remarks-president-obama-memorial-service-former-south-african-president-, published 10 December 2013, accessed 5 July 2022.

Pearce, C. L., Conger, J. A., & Locke, E. A. (2007). Shared leadership theory. *The Leadership Quarterly, 18*(3), 281–288.

Pearce, J. (2019). Jurgen Klopp exclusive: When we start a team meeting the only thing I really know I am going to say is the first sentence. https://theathletic.com/1384977/2019/11/21/jurgen-klopp-exclusive-when-we-start-a-team-meeting-the-only-thing-i-really-know-i-am-going-to-say-is-the-first-sentence/, published 21 November 2019, accessed 30 June 2022.

Pendleton, D., & Furnham, A. F. (2016). *Leadership: All You Need to Know*, 2nd ed. London: Palgrave Macmillan.

Pfeffer, J., & Salancik, G. R. (2003). *The External Control of Organizations: A Resource Dependence Perspective.* Stanford, CA: Stanford University Press.

Pinkley, R. L. (1990). Dimensions of conflict frame: Disputant interpretations of conflict. *Journal of Applied Psychology, 75*(2), 117–126.

Pittino, D., Visintin, F., & Compagno, C. (2018). Co-leadership and performance in technology-based entrepreneurial firms. In: Cubico, S., Favretto, Leitão, J., & Canter, U. (eds), *Entrepreneurship and the Industry Life Cycle* (pp. 91–106). Cham: Springer.

Quigley, T. J., & Hambrick, D. C. (2015). Has the "CEO effect" increased in recent decades? A new explanation for the great rise in America's attention to corporate leaders. *Strategic Management Journal, 36*(6), 821–830.

Resick, C. J., Whitman, D. S., Weingarden, S. M., & Hiller, N. J. (2009). The bright-side and the dark-side of CEO personality: Examining core self-evaluations, narcissism, transformational leadership, and strategic influence. *Journal of Applied Psychology, 94*(6), 1365–1381.

Rittel, H. W., & Webber, M. M. (1973). Dilemmas in a general theory of planning. *Policy Sciences, 4*(2), 155–169.

Roberts, B. W., & DelVecchio, W. F. (2000). The rank-order consistency of personality traits from childhood to old age: A quantitative review of longitudinal studies. *Psychological Bulletin, 126*(1), 3–25.

Rowe, A. J., & Boulgarides, J. D. (1992). *Managerial Decision Making*. New York, NY: Macmillan Publishing Company.

Ruben, B. D., & Gigliotti, R. A. (2016). Leadership as social influence: An expanded view of leadership communication theory and practice. *Journal of Leadership & Organizational Studies, 23*(4), 467–479.

Rucci, A. J., Kirn, S. P., & Quinn, R. T. (1998). The employee-customer-profit chain at Sears. *Harvard Business Review, 76*(1), 82–98.

Salovey, P., & Mayer, J. D. (1990). Emotional intelligence. *Imagination, Cognition and Personality, 9*(3), 185–211.

Sandberg, S., & Grant, A. (2017). *Option B: Facing Adversity, Building Resilience, and Finding Joy*. New York, NY: Penguin.

Sandberg, S., Matloff Goler, L., & McGee, D. (2017). There have been many times … https://www.facebook.com/sheryl/posts/10158115250050177, published February 7 2022, accessed 25 July 2022.

Schein, E. H. (1996). Kurt Lewin's change theory in the field and in the classroom: Notes toward a model of managed learning. *Systems Practice, 9*(1), 27–47.

Schein, E. H. (2010). *Organizational Culture and Leadership*, 4th ed. San Francisco, CA: Jossey-Bass.

Simonet, D. V., & Tett, R. P. (2013). Five perspectives on the leadership–management relationship: A competency-based evaluation and integration. *Journal of Leadership & Organizational Studies, 20*(2), 199–213.

Smith, M. A., & Canger, J. M. (2004). Effects of supervisor 'big five' personality on subordinate attitudes. *Journal of Business and Psychology, 18*(4), 465–481.

Sternad, D. (2020). Lead like Klopp. Macmillan Higher Education MIHE Blog. https://www.macmillanihe.com/blog/post/lead-like-klopp-management-sternad/, published 21 July 2020, accessed 1 August 2020.

Sternad D. (2021). *Developing Coaching Skills: A Concise Introduction*. Moosburg: econcise.

Sternad, D. (2021a). *Solve It! The Mindset and Tools of Smart Problem Solvers*. Moosburg: econcise.

Stogdill, R. M. (1969). Validity of leader behavior descriptions. *Personnel Psychology, 22*(2), 153–158.

Stogdill, R. M. (1974). *Handbook of Leadership: A Survey of Theory and Research*. New York, NY: Free Press.

Taylor III, A. (2009). Fixing up Ford. https://archive.fortune.com/2009/05/11/news/companies/ mulally_ford.fortune/index.htm, published 12 May 2009, accessed 5 July 2022.

theguardian.com (2015). Jürgen Klopp promises to deliver 'full throttle' football at Liverpool, https://www.theguardian.com/football/2015/oct/09/liverpool-jurgen-klopp-full-throt- tle-football, published 9 October 2015, accessed 30 June 2022.

Thomas, K. W. (1976). Conflict and conflict management. In: Dunnette, M. (ed.), *Handbook of Industrial and Organizational Psychology* (pp. 889–935). Chicago: Rand McNally.

Townsend, J., Phillips, J. S., & Elkins, T. J. (2000). Employee retaliation: The neglected conse- quence of poor leader–member exchange relations. *Journal of Occupational Health Psychology, 5*(4), 457–463.

Tribelhorn, M. (2021). Mario Corti tried to save Swissair – and became a scapegoat. Twenty years later, he tells his side of the story. https://www.nzz.ch/english/swissairs-last-ceo-mario- corti-breaks-his-silence-ld.1648788, published 7 October 2021, accessed 28 June 2022.

Trompenaars, A., & Hampden-Turner, C. (2012). *Riding the Waves of Culture: Understanding Culture and Diversity in Business.* New York, NY: McGraw Hill

Van Knippenberg, D., & Stam, D. (2014). Visionary leadership. In: Day, D. V. (ed.), *The Oxford Handbook of Leadership and Organizations* (pp. 241–259). Oxford: Oxford University Press.

Van Minh, N., Badir, Y. F., Quang, N. N., & Afsar, B. (2017). The impact of leaders' technical competence on employees' innovation and learning. *Journal of Engineering and Technology Management, 44,* 44–57.

Vroom, V. H., & Yetton, P. W. (1973). *Leadership and Decision Making.* Pittsburgh, PA: University of Pittsburgh Press.

Vroom, V. H., & Jago, A. G. (1988). *The New Leadership: Managing Participation in Organizations.* Englewood Cliffs, NJ: Prentice Hall.

Washington Post (January 21 1969, page A01). Richard M. Nixon becomes President with 'sacred commitment' to peace. https://www.washingtonpost.com/wp-srv/national/longterm/ inaug/history/stories/nixon69.htm, accessed 5 July 2022.

Whitmore, J. H. D. (2010). *Coaching for Performance: The Principles and Practice of Coaching and Leadership.* London: Hachette UK.

Witt, L. A., Burke, L. A., Barrick, M. R., & Mount, M. K. (2002). The interactive effects of con- scientiousness and agreeableness on job performance. *Journal of Applied Psychology, 87*(1), 164–169.

Yukl, G., Mahsud, R., Hassan, S., & Prussia, G. E. (2013). An improved measure of ethical leadership. *Journal of Leadership & Organizational Studies, 20*(1), 38–48.

Yukl, G. (2013). *Leadership in Organizations,* 8th ed. Boston, MA: Pearson Education.

Yukl, G., & Gardner III, William L. (2020). *Leadership in Organizations,* 9th ed. Harlow: Pearson Education.

Zaccaro, S. J. (2001). Organizational leadership and social intelligence. In: Riggio, R. E., Mur- phy, S. E., & Pirozzolo, F. J. (eds.) *Multiple Intelligences and Leadership* (pp. 42–68). New York, NY: Psychology Press.

Zaccaro, S. J., Mumford, M. D., Connelly, M. S., Marks, M. A., & Gilbert, J. A. (2000). Assess- ment of leader problem-solving capabilities. *The Leadership Quarterly, 11*(1), 37–64.

Index

H

Hall, Edward T. 85
Hampden-Turner, Charles 85
Hersey, Paul 11
Hofstede, Geert 85, 86
'How to lead' matrix 57
Huawei 79
humane orientation (cultural
    dimension) 86
humane-oriented leadership 87
human skills 35-37

I

idealized influence 68
inclusion 84, 98-99
individualism 85
individualized consideration 69
influence 7
in-group 13, 61-64
integrity 94
intellectual stimulation 69
interaction between leader and
    followers 12
interpersonal skills 37-39
introverts 28
invisible leadership 70

J

Jago, Arthur G. 121
Jobs, Steve 118
joint leadership 6, 77 *see also shared*
    leadership
Jung, Carl G. 31

K

Klopp, Jürgen 75-76
Kotter, John P. 100-101, 104

L

laissez-faire style 10, 49, 52, 58
leader, definition 6
leader-follower relationship 12,
    55-56, 58-61, 66-67
leader–member exchange (LMX)
    model 13, 61-62, 65
leadership and management 20, 22
leadership
  as a process 6
  as social construction 13
  behavior 9, 45
  communication 110
  definition 6
  development plan 132, 134
  effectiveness 60
  grid (Blake and Mouton) 45
  skills 32
  speech 112
leadership styles 9, 11, 45-46, 105
  self-assessment exercise 47
  emotional 12
leaders' values 12
leading across cultures 84
leading change 100-101
  agile approach 104
leading teams 73
leading virtual teams 90
Lewin, Kurt 9, 48, 100
Liverpool FC 75-76
LMX theory *see leader-member*
    exchange model

M

management 15, 20
masculinity (cultural dimension) 85
Mayer, John 39
McKee, Anne 12, 105
McKinsey & Company 65

Daniel Pittino is a management professor with extensive teaching experience in leadership at undergraduate and graduate levels, as well as at an executive level. He has long acted as an advisor for strategic leaders in entrepreneurial firms, and has written textbooks and book chapters for various international publishers (including McGraw Hill, Emerald and Sage). Several of his research articles are featured in top-tier journals within the field of management.

Printed in the USA
CPSIA information can be obtained
at www.ICGtesting.com
LVHW051104180224
772143LV00005B/672